The Clinician's Guide to Medical Cannabis

Matthew Roman, MD

For Fay.

CONTENTS

	Introduction	i
1	The Basics	1
2	The Patient Physician Relationship	11
3	The Patient Encounter	18
4	Side Effects	23
5	Dose and Types	28
6	Dispensaries and Inpatients	36
7	Primary Care	40
8	Pain Management	46
9	Other Conditions	51

INTRODUCTION

There are countless courses online about medical marijuana, but they all have similar information in them. They begin with a detailed history of marijuana prohibition and the passage of the 1970 Controlled Substances Act (CSA), which officially prohibited the use of cannabis for any purpose and prevented its research. This is followed by a discussion of the endocannabinoid system on a theoretical level and, finally, an explanation of cannabis-related disorders (i.e., cannabinoid hyperemesis syndrome).

Unfortunately, these courses provide little guidance to clinicians on a practical level. Time and time again I have heard physicians say, "I understand the endocannabinoid system, but when a patient asks me for recommendations on what to use, I don't know what to tell them." Healthcare providers who work in a clinical setting need practical answers; that is what this guide seeks to provide.

We are entering a new era in medicine that appreciates the benefits of tetrahydrocannabinol (THC), the active compound in marijuana. It is a wild-wild-west as we attempt to use this drug for healing purposes despite a relative absence of scientific literature on the subject. Claims of all sorts are being purported by the growing cannabis industry and the FDA, a federal agency, is not checking them. A list of constituents found in cannabis are being credited for its therapeutic benefits, such as CBD, CBV and terpenes. This creates confusion and muddies the waters for doctors and their patients.

In this situation, it is best to have a skeptical outlook. As scientists, we have to understand the Scientific Method and remind ourselves that not all studies are equal. The lack of government funding for cannabis research has left us with few, privately funded studies that are usually of low power and minimal significance. Worse, many are inherently biased – either seeking to prove that cannabis is inherently harmful or that a particular product is beneficial. In today's scientific databases, it is possible to find studies that are positive and negative for the same treatments. Anyone can find research to support their preconceived ideas and beliefs. Yet the trend in pseudoscientific modalities is one where early low-power studies are positive and with time larger studies disprove the initial research. We are at this first phase of scientific discovery in cannabis. There are small research studies claiming benefits to various chemicals within cannabis and it is only through a skeptic's glasses that we can see the truth more clearly.

Tetrahydrocannabinol (THC) is a remarkable medicine with a diverse therapeutic profile unlike any other drug. Unlike standard medications that target specific cellular functions, cannabis restores homeostasis throughout the body and mind. It is almost a panacea because it directly treats or alleviates symptoms of both acute and chronic pathology in almost every major organ system and the psyche. It has properties that are beneficial for treating inflammation, pain, autoimmunity, insomnia, grief, depression, PTSD, failure to thrive, cancer, neuropathy, nausea, obesity, epilepsy, alcoholism, and opiate withdrawal.

Dispensaries across the world are providing patients with new varieties of medical marijuana products. Meanwhile, physicians receive mixed messages from the federal government, our employers and our patients. Even between ourselves, there is no consensus on how to approach marijuana. Most major medical associations are against the use of cannabis to treat patients' illnesses mostly because of a "lack of research." The research isn't there because the government blocks it, not because of a lack of benefit.

Patients have been using medical cannabis without the approval of physicians for millennia.[1] We have reached a strange circumstance due to its prohibition and the absence of research, where the patients are more knowledgeable about cannabis use than their doctors. We therefore have to admit to our shortcomings and learn from the patients. I happen to be one such patient and have used marijuana extensively throughout my life. I have also specialized in the practical use of cannabis in a primary care setting for almost the entirety of my career as an independent practitioner and I have written this guide to teach other providers about cannabis in a way that will give them a clearer understanding of what to say to patients when instructing them.

This guide begins by teaching the basic "street-smarts" that patients already know but doctors do not. Without this foundation, physicians will always seem "out of the loop" about cannabis to their experienced patients. Afterwards, the discussion of new, more advanced forms and methods of treatment will ensue. Finally, we will apply what we learned about these methods of cannabis use to the clinic and learn treatment strategies for specific diseases and clinical scenarios.

The information you will learn will equip you with the know-how to provide recommendations for patients in your own practices so that you can become specialists of medical cannabis within your respective fields.

---

[1] Li HL. An Archaeological and Historical Account of Cannabis in China. *Econ Bot.* 1974;28(4): 444.

1 THE BASICS

"Recreational" vs "Medical"

The term "recreational" marijuana has in the past generally been used to mean illegal use of marijuana. Once patients were able to use cannabis with the guidance of a doctor and according to state laws, the use of marijuana became "medical." However, just because marijuana is legal does not mean it can't be used recreationally and vice versa- if it is illegal, that does not mean it cannot be used for medical purposes. More recently, states have legalized marijuana use without the need for a physician, and this has been termed recreational marijuana. Many patients purchasing marijuana this way are still using it for medical purposes, they just do so without the guidance of a physician. To me, it is almost all medical use because patients who use cannabis typically do so to relieve anxiety and stress.

Marijuana's prohibition was a political phenomenon, not a scientific one. The medical community had no say in the matter. Unlike drugs like cocaine and heroin, the high of marijuana is not pleasurable. Actually, it's rather uncomfortable and can cause anxiety and paranoia. However, patients choose to accept these side effects and the risk of criminal prosecution because the therapeutic benefits exceed these negatives. The relief of using marijuana is greater than its unwanted side effects.

Cannabis is a self-limiting drug that pushes users away from further use once a patient is medicated. Other drugs are a slippery slope towards overdose because users happily use more of them after consuming an initial quantity. For these reasons, cannabis is usually used as a therapeutic medication rather than a drug of abuse. Aside from rare circumstances and nascent experimentation, cannabis is usually used as "medical" rather than "recreational" marijuana.

Nomenclature

Cannabis sativa is the Latin taxonomy of the plant species. Both medical and industrial forms of this plant fall under the name Cannabis. When it is grown for food and industrial purposes, like fabric or paper, it is referred to as *hemp*. The term *marijuana* denotes cultivars that are grown for its therapeutic properties – including the high it produces.

These terms can be occasionally confusing and incorrectly used. Hemp has in recent years been considered legal whereas marijuana has traditionally been outlawed. Since hemp includes the nutritional components of *Cannabis sativa*, edible oil derived from *Cannabis sativa* is often called hemp oil. However, the CBD industry has been using the term *hemp* to insinuate that their products are legal. Since, by federal law, hemp must contain no more than 0.3% THC, a product that is called 'CBD hemp oil' suggests that it does not contain THC even though it is being sold for its purported therapeutic benefits, regardless of the authenticity of those claims.

Ultimately, hemp lacks THC and, as we will later learn, has very little therapeutic value, if any. For this reason, it should be reserved for describing marijuana that is for industrial purposes, not therapeutic. On the other hand, cannabis that is cultivated for its active ingredient, THC, should be called "marijuana."

There has been a trend in the cannabis community to refrain from using the term "marijuana" because it is derived from the original spelling "marihuana" and was used to villainize the drug by the US government by insinuating a Mexican origin. The species itself is indigenous to eastern Asia but linking it to Mexico was a racist propaganda plot to slander the drug and turn the public against it. Still, this new spelling has been adopted for decades and rather than using the term hemp or cannabis in its place, we should either return to the classic spelling of *marihuana* or accept the now popular spelling *marijuana* rather than referring to it as cannabis, which lacks specificity of industrial vs therapeutic purpose.

Patients have many street terms for marijuana. The most common name is *weed*. Other names include *bud, ganja, reefer, 420, grass, chronic*. High-quality marijuana is more recently called *loud* and low-quality marijuana is called *shwag* and *reggie*, which contains seeds in the product.

Most marijuana is seedless, and the term *sensimilla* means seedless in Spanish. Seeds occur when cannabis male plants are allowed to pollinate female plants. Properly grown marijuana is from female plants only that have been separated from any males and prevented from being pollinated by them.

Cannabis sativa has leaves and flowers, but the marijuana portion itself is now called *flower*, even though it has no botanical relation to the flower portion of the plant. The same goes for the term *bud*. There are no actual buds, (as in the compact growth on a plant that develops into shoots and leaves) in marijuana "flower." For the purposes of simplicity, we will adhere to the popular term *flower* for the therapeutically usable part of cannabis even though it is not an actual flower.

Appearance

Marijuana flower is the fruit of the cannabis plant that grows at the top of its stalks. Leaves are trimmed off of it by machines or people designated as *trimmers*. It does not have the appearance of fruit but rather looks like a spongy, green mossy substance with small hairs. It has a fine, sugar-coated appearance on close inspection, which is caused by organelles containing THC called *trichomes*. It's consistency ranges from light and fluffy to dense and firm. It can be soft and moist when fresh but will dry out to a crisp if left to sit out in the open.

Professionals "cure" their products after an initial drying period to improve consistency and enhance its aroma and taste. Potent strains are sticky to the touch from the THC "crystals" oozing from the trichomes. The color is generally green but the hairs on the outside of the marijuana can be orange, red, and white. Strains with purple hues are becoming increasingly popular.

Products that are made by extracting THC from marijuana look entirely different and will be discussed in more detail later in this guide.

Distribution

In the eighties, marijuana was imported from Mexico and South America and was sold on the streets in nickel-bags (nick bags) and dime-bags for five and ten dollars, respectively. This was enough to roll into a marijuana cigarette, which typically contains about one gram of marijuana flower. In the nineties, prices and quality of marijuana went up and the cost rose to $20 per gram and was commonly sold in increments of an ounce. An eighth of an ounce (3.5 grams) would cost about $40 dollars and today's boutique dispensaries charge sometimes upwards of $60 per eight. In the future, this will deflate to almost zero once patients can grow marijuana in on their own legally. In the state of Oregon, the cost of an ounce of marijuana has already dropped to just $15 dollars on the streets.

Methods of Use

The most common method of using marijuana is smoking. Traditionally, the flower is crushed or ground up in a grinder and rolled into marijuana cigarettes, called *joints*, using rolling papers. Urban communities popularized a similar version of smoking called a blunt. Instead of using thin, white rolling papers, they would crack a cigar down the middle and use the exterior leaf to roll marijuana flower. This adds a nicotine rush from the tobacco and can hold more marijuana inside so that it lasts longer and can be passed around in a group to more people. Smoking a blunt communally was a way for urban groups to medicate together and provide psychological relief from shared oppression. Authorities would consider this criminal activity but, in many ways, it was a kind of group therapy that was occurring rather than recreation.

The other way to smoke marijuana is through a pipe. Glass is the preferred material because it's easier to clean and does not conduct heat from the flame of the lighter or the ember (called a *cherry*) once it is burning. The part of the pipe that is filled with marijuana is called the *bowl* and after it is packed with product, a flame from a lighter can be drawn through it producing smoke that is inhaled. Most glass pipes have a hole called a *shotgun* on their side that is covered during inhalation and released to clear out the left-over smoke inside the pipe.

Large waterpipes called *bongs* are designed with enough dead space in them to match our lungs' vital capacity. Two inhalations are needed – one to "milk" the waterpipe, filling it full of smoke, and one to clear out the smoke and inhale it into the lungs. This allows for a much larger volume of smoke to be inhaled that delivers more THC into the body at once.

Waterpipes have bowls attached to *downstems* that extend below the waterline in the lower chamber of the pipe. Smoke is percolated through the water to cool it and cleanse it from some of the water-soluble byproducts. The lipophilic properties of THC allow it to pass through the water and stay in the smoke until it reaches the alveoli and is deposited rapidly into the surfactant layer. From there, it is transported in the bloodstream to the body over a period of minutes. The effects are felt immediately and last about two hours.

A cleaner way to inhale marijuana is with vaporization instead of smoking it. Rather than combusting the product with a flame, marijuana flower can be finely ground and packed into an electronic vaporizer device that heats air to a temperature just below the temperature that would set the marijuana on fire[2] and create smoke. As hot air is inhaled and pulled through the marijuana, THC evaporates into a vapor or mist.

Vaporization of marijuana flower (*vaping for short*) has been a favorite method of cancer patients to use cannabis. The inhaled vapor is less irritating to the airways than smoke and contains less tar. An expensive but well-made product from Germany, called the Volcano, is a desktop appliance that has been the gold-standard for vaporizing cannabis. It pre-fills a clear plastic bag with vapor that can be easily detached and inhaled from like a balloon. Inexpensive flower vaporizers are usually inefficient, so vaporizing dried cannabis flower is less popular than smoking it overtly. This may change as the cost of cannabis decreases.

In recent years, vaporizing non-flower cannabis products has boomed in popularity. *Vape-pens*, as they are called, contain an oily liquid mixture usually containing propylene glycol and vegetable glycerol that has a high percentage of THC extracted from marijuana flower. These devices are rechargeable or have disposable batteries and produce no odor. Like flower vaporization, they are far less irritating to the lungs than smoke is. In the future, this will likely become the most common method of medicating with marijuana for the typical patient.

Having discussed the inhaled versions of marijuana, now let's turn to oral cannabis products. Cannabis flower contains THCA (tetrahydrocannabinolic acid), which is physiologically inactive until it is heated to the correct temperature and decarboxylated into THC. Very little THCA is converted to THC in vivo so it does not have utility as a prodrug.[3]

---

[2] The boiling point of THC is approximately 400°F (392°F or 200°C at 0.02mm Hg pressure).

[3] Moreno-Sanz G. Can You Pass the Acid Test? Critical Review and Novel Therapeutic

The reason inhaled products administer THC is that their THCA is heated to the temperature at which decarboxylation occurs during vaporization or combustion. Oral cannabis products, on the other hand, have to be either infused with pre-decarboxylated THC or baked in an oven to decarboxylate their THCA, like in "magic brownies" that contain marijuana.

Oral ingestion of THC has a completely different effect than inhalation. The onset of action can take up to two hours because THC is highly lipophilic and probably absorbed with lipids and cholesterol in chylomicrons and then secreted into the bloodstream through the lymphatic system at the thoracic duct. This results in a lower concentration peak, but the duration of effects lasts about five hours,[4] instead of the usual two hours after inhaling THC. The effect is often described as a "body high," possibly a result of THC's metabolism to 11-Hydroxy-THC in the liver, which is also physiologically active.

The most common method of preparing edible marijuana involves cooking it on low heat in butter for a couple hours to allow it to decarboxylate. The flower grounds are strained out and the butter can be used as an ingredient in other recipes. The same can be done with cooking oil.

Concentrates

Marijuana is covered in THC-containing trichomes that feel sticky and can be collected at the bottom of containers in the form of a powder, called *kief*. This is the most basic form of concentrate and can be made by patients in their home. *Grinders* for marijuana often have a screen at the bottom of them that lets kief develop as trichomes fall through and collect into a powder. This can be sprinkled into joints and onto bowls to increase potency.

Perspectives of Δ9-Tetrahydrocannabinolic Acid A. *Cannabis Cannabinoid Res.* 2016;1(1):124-130. doi:10.1089/can.2016.0008. PMC 5549534. PMID 28861488.

[4] Huestis MA. Pharmacokinetics and metabolism of the plant cannabinoids, delta9-tetrahydrocannabinol, cannabidiol and cannabinol. *Handb Exp Pharmacol.* 2005;168:657–90. doi:10.1007/3-540-26573-2_23. PMID 16596792.

Kief can be used to create a black, pliable putty called *hashish*, or "hash" for short. Hashish is also made in Asia and the Middle East by handling marijuana and rubbing the sticky residue that forms on the hands into small pliable balls. It contains a high percentage of THC and can be added to tobacco or marijuana. It's popularity in America has been less than in Europe and other parts of the world.

Sometime during the end of the 20th century, a more refined concentrate was developed, called Butane Hash Oil (BHO). This was created by packing pipes with ground marijuana and passing butane through them. The non-polar gas acts as a solvent that dissolves the THC and other cannabinoids into an amber-colored sauce that drips out of the end of the pipe. Once dried, it solidifies into concentrates that are marketed with different names based on their consistency. For example, brittle versions are called *shatter* and softer ones *wax*.

Meanwhile, in Canada, a man named Rick Simpson began dissolving marijuana in ethanol and carefully cooking off the alcohol. The remaining oil was high in THC and used to treat cancer in patients who were his friends and loved ones. He felt that the results were so beneficial that he went public, exposing himself and his activities. Since then, alcohol-extracted THC products have been called Rick Simpson Oil ("R.S.O.") and considered by many to be the best form of cannabis to treat cancer. Workers at dispensaries called *budtenders* advise patients on which products to buy and often recommend Rick Simpson oil to cancer patients. RSO is usually an edible product because THCA is decarboxylated into THC when the alcohol is boiled out of the product. It is called an "oil" but its consistency is sticky and more similar to a honey or molasses than oil. Home-made RSO is dark, even black in color but industry produced RSO is the color of honey.

Another method for creating extracts was found by squeezing cannabis flower tightly between two sides of a hair straightener using a vise. The heat from the hair straighteners warms the flower enough to squeeze out a sap called *rosin*. This form of concentrate has more flavor because it contains more *terpenes* – a large and diverse class of aromatic organic compounds, often touted as having medicinal properties. Since it does not require extraction with a solvent, it is considered to be one of the most natural concentrates. After this technique was discovered, commercial "rosin-presses" have been manufactured that are designed to squeeze cannabis flower at higher pressures with exact temperature control. Some of these presses are marketed to the regular consumer, others for industrial purposes.

Distilled versions of marijuana concentrates are called *distillates*. They are the result of laboratory distillation techniques that purify constituents of cannabis flower and mix them together in specific proportions. Most commonly, purified THC or CBD is used as the base and then a "sauce" is added that contains known amounts of terpenes. Often times these products are said to be "full-spectrum" because they contain a wide array of additives, which have no clinical value compared to the active ingredient THC. The extraction process usually involves liquid CO_2, which results in *CO_2-oil*, a less viscous concentrate that is more liquid than solid, like other concentrates.

Purified THC or THCA is a crystalline solid. When added to sauce, manufacturers call it *crystals*. Alone, it is called *diamonds*. This is the most prized form of medical marijuana because it is 100% active ingredient and contains no unnecessary byproducts or additives. It can be vaporized in both THC and THCA forms but works as an edible only if it is decarboxylated THC.

Vaporizing Marijuana Concentrates

Concentrates can be vaporized in special vaporizers manufactured for use with wax, though other concentrates will work too (except hashish and kief). They are engineered with similar parts. An *atomizer* contains wire heating coils in a vapor chamber. The wires of the coil are wrapped around a cotton wick or some ceramic material. Cotton wick absorbs concentrate more effectively into the coils but has a shorter lifespan. The atomizer and its coils sit inside a vapor chamber so that concentrates can be applied to the atomizer and are contained and protected from splashing or boiling over while vaporizing. The most cost-effective example of this kind of device uses a glass bulb for the chamber and a porcelain atomizer with cotton wicks. All of these devices are rechargeable with a lithium ion battery that screws in.

The other method of vaporizing concentrates is by far the most powerful way of medicating with cannabis – colloquially called *dabbing*. Glass pipes called *oil rigs* are equipped with a titanium or quartz attachment called a *nail* that is pre-heated for concentrates that are applied directly to its surface.

Nails are heated either electronically ("e-nail") with a coil similar to those on old-fashioned electric stove tops or using a torch.

Nails designed for heating with a torch are called *bangers* and are made of quartz glass, which can sustain the rapid temperature changes of torching and cooling. Quartz bangers are shaped like a mug because they have a flat bottom that is thicker and can store more heat. Establishing the right temperature using a quartz nail is a skill. If the banger is too hot, the concentrate will burn and leave a black residue. If the temperature is too low, the concentrate will not vaporize. Typically, a torch is applied to the bottom of the banger for 30-60 seconds and allowed to cool for one to two minutes. Theoretically, the optimal temperature to reach is slightly above the boiling point of THC, which is 160 C (320F). Patients can purchase special thermometers to check the temperature of the banger before they use it or learn through trial and error how long to heat and cool it. E-nails are more consistent in this regard because they can be digitally controlled and set to an exact temperature.

After the nail is heated to the right temperature, marijuana concentrates are "dabbed" with a small glass or metal stick into the nail. A special glass cap (called a *carb cap*) is placed on top of the nail to direct air at the concentrates and vaporize it more efficiently. The highest doses of marijuana can be consumed this way because the percentage of THC in concentrates is usually 60% or higher, so a 100mg amount dabbed delivers 60mg or more of THC in one inhalation. In comparison, a joint from 1 gram of 20% THC marijuana flower has 200mg of THC, so two dabs is like smoking half of the joint in two inhalations. A dab can be very tiny, like the size of a poppyseed, or, in extreme cases, a gram or more (though this is not appropriate from a medical standpoint and almost certainly qualifies as recreational use).

The lower the percentage of THC in the concentrate, the more residue will be left behind to clean from the nail. It is a remarkable experience to drop 100% THC diamonds into a banger and watch it vaporize completely without leaving behind any residue. The resultant vapor that is inhaled has the least byproducts and additional flavors and tastes the cleanest and smoothest.

Topicals

Topical marijuana products have been researched very little but may have significant therapeutic properties. THC is extremely lipophilic and hydrophobic, making it an excellent candidate for dermatologic absorption. As we eagerly await double-blinded studies to determine its efficacy as a topical, it is safe to assume that at least some of it is absorbed and has local effects. It is a wonder that such studies haven't been performed because of federal prohibition. Certainly, the potential benefits of topical THC far outweigh the risk of recommending this to patients, even in the absence of research. It has no systemic effects, so it does not cause the psychoactive high, but it may provide anti-inflammatory and analgesic local properties.

2 THE PATIENT PHYSICIAN RELATIONSHIP

Using Marijuana as a Physician

The fastest way to understand marijuana is to become a patient and experience it personally. Even the healthiest individuals occasionally suffer from anxiety, insomnia and pain. It's always best to adhere closely to state laws and policies regarding marijuana use. Most states allow medical cannabis now. Providing paperwork to a physician that can certify you for a medical marijuana card will allow you to see what your state's dispensaries are selling patients and you can try these products for yourself. If you live in a state that does not have medical marijuana, take a vacation to one that has recreational marijuana. The reason I recommend this is that no physician can understand marijuana completely without experiencing it personally.

I must provide a strong warning, however, to any physicians courageous enough to attempt this experience. Even if a medical marijuana card is acquired by a physician, that information should be kept as confidential as possible. There is a stigma against physicians using cannabis, even for medical purposes in their own homes. The medical boards and Departments of Professional Regulations have a responsibility to determine if physicians are safe to perform their profession and there is a financial incentive to diagnose them with a substance use disorder.

If they suspect that a physician is using cannabis, even legally as a treatment of a condition, they will demand an evaluation by a physician of their choice, whose job it is to label us with a Cannabis Use Disorder. Once this happens, we are placed in rehab centers alongside alcoholics and opioid addicts. Maintaining our ability to work with our licenses on probation requires weekly drug testing and therapy, workplace monitors, attendance at Alcoholics Anonymous meetings, and monitoring by a physician that has completed their program, amongst other requirements. This is against the laws protecting patients who treat their illnesses with medical marijuana, but the state medical boards do not care.

Using cannabis as a physician is a risky endeavor but I have approved dozens of MDs and DOs for cannabis cards and they have all received therapeutic benefit from it. None of them have had licensure problems because they kept their treatment confidential. Physicians who have experienced the effects of marijuana are more cognizant of what to tell their patients when recommending cannabis. Don't be discouraged if you are not willing to take that risk. This guide's purpose is to equip physicians with the know-how to feel comfortable recommending marijuana to their own patients even if they haven't tried it themselves.

"Prescribing" Marijuana

A quick note about the ability to prescribe marijuana to patients. Technically, federal law prevents any healthcare provider from prescribing a schedule 1 substance to patients, because by definition these substances have no medical benefit (so they claim). This, of course, is not true in the case of marijuana (and probably other Schedule 1 substances) but the state laws define them this way anyway.

To protect physicians from federal jurisdictions, states have devised a way around this technicality: patients receive medical marijuana cards instead of prescriptions. The card serves a similar purpose to a prescription because it provides the access to medical cannabis using a physician's approval. It is different in that the physician can not specify an exact dose or form of marijuana to be used. Given the general ignorance and lack of cannabis education by doctors, this is probably a good thing. Patients are recommended specific strains and types of medical marijuana by budtenders at dispensaries when purchasing marijuana. They are allowed to choose their own products if they decline to take the recommendations of budtenders.

As physicians, we don't "prescribe" marijuana, we *certify* patients for marijuana cards and *recommend* specific types of products. The advice we provide to patients during our appointments holds the most weight and patients will challenge what they are told at dispensaries if it does not coincide with their physician's recommendations. Giving patients the wrong advice can have long-lasting consequences and delay appropriate marijuana treatment. In other situations, it can result in adverse effects and overdoses. For this reason, it is advisable to educate oneself on the best practices as described in this book.

Providing Support for Patients

There are many sociopolitical circumstances where patients need the support of a physician after they are recommended medical marijuana. Starting with the patient's family, relatives can be against the use of marijuana and make it difficult for the patient to begin treatment. In such situations, it is advisable to help convince the family otherwise. Without the family's approval, it is usually impossible for the patient to start treatment or continue it in adequate amounts. Such situations call for the physician to write a letter documenting the reasons why the patient may benefit from marijuana so the family can read it for themselves. Have a close discussion with the patient about their family's concerns and address them directly in the letter. Addressing the family's concerns can alleviate them and open the door to medical marijuana treatment for the patient. When the family reads the letter, they will be more accepting of the patient's marijuana use at home.

Patients who are on probation will often have push back from their parole officers, who drug test them and intimidate them or lie to them by saying they are not legally allowed to use cannabis. In states where cannabis is legal, this is definitely not true. In my experience, parole officers' attitudes about marijuana use by their parolees varies on a case by case basis. Some refer their parolees to get a marijuana card, so they are using it legally and are not punished for it. Others are totally against it. In the worst situations, patients have been wrongfully arrested for their medical marijuana use. This can be prevented by providing supplemental documentation declaring THC initiation, confirming its necessity, and assuring close monitoring. Specifying the patient's diagnosis is not necessary and respects their HIPAA rights. Sometimes, giving the exact diagnosis (e.g., chronic pain, anxiety, etc.) gives room for scrutiny by the parole officer, who may not believe their condition is severe enough to warrant marijuana. Nevertheless, a letter from a physician helps parole officers accept the need for a patient's medical marijuana treatment.

Employment drug screens usually call for a letter by the certifying physician. Showing a medical marijuana card to the HR department is often not enough to appease employers fearing that their employees are using marijuana illegally. Some employers haven't adjusted to shifting cannabis laws and threaten termination without a letter of support or paperwork from the certifying doctor.

As certifying providers who recommend medical marijuana, it is our duty to prevent patient job loss by writing an official letter of support that explains the patient's compliance with our recommendations. Noting that proper treatment may enhance a patient's effectiveness in the workplace can be helpful. Remember to say that the patient does not use marijuana while they are at work and don't forget to counsel patients on this at their appointments. This is especially true for high-risk jobs (heavy machinery, driving, medical responsibilities, etc.). Writing a letter of support for the patient will assure you that any subsequent job loss was not because you certified them to use marijuana and instead more likely to be because of other reasons, like office politics or poor performance. Be careful with patients who are federal employees, especially federal law enforcement. An FBI agent, for example, is not going to be allowed to use marijuana because the federal government still considers it unlawful, regardless of state laws.

Other circumstances for physician letters of support arise when patients travel to other states where marijuana is medically legal. Since patients require state-provided cannabis cards to receive medication, patients from out-of-state can't access treatment. However, some states have allowed out-of-state patients to circumvent this problem by providing a letter from their doctor stating their diagnosis and that they have been recommended marijuana treatment for it. Jamaica also allows Americans to purchase medical marijuana from their dispensaries with a doctor's letter. Providing letters of support will ensure that traveling patients will not have an abrupt cessation in treatment and can continue using medical cannabis legally. Patients will have less risk of breaking laws by carrying cannabis across borders or searching for it on the black market. They will be able to leave their cannabis at home and purchase new cannabis to use in the state they travel to, if that is allowed there with a letter from their physician.

Rarely, patients may need paperwork for colleges to justify their marijuana possession in dormitories. Expect other situations to arise that also need a letter of support or paperwork filled out as more institutions and organizations become accepting of cannabis use for medical purposes. The shifting laws will call for our adaptability to new circumstances that require our support of patients.

Patient-Physician Relationship

Patients are afraid to discuss their marijuana use with their doctors. Well over half of my patients admit to using less marijuana on their written appointment intake forms than they reveal upon a close personal discussion. Historically, marijuana prohibition was a political endeavor that wasn't grounded in science. The American Medical Association was unsupportive of initial attempts to prohibit marijuana by the government.[5] Today, most physicians believe the propaganda that villainizes cannabis use despite its low risk to health and many medical benefits. This proves that physicians are basing their opinions of marijuana on sociopolitical views instead of sound medical science. The result is that these physicians view patients like criminals for using cannabis. To treat patients this way is criminal itself. Patients are afraid to even breach the subject of cannabis with their doctors out of fear of being criticized and insulted.

To counter the fear that patients have of discussing cannabis use with doctors, physicians can take-on a general feeling of regret about the situation that the patients have been put in. Physicians should be regretful that it has taken the medical community this long to seriously consider cannabis as a legitimate medical treatment. We should even feel ashamed for perpetuating the propaganda around cannabis for so many decades. To this day medical organizations disagree with the acceptance of cannabis as a legitimate treatment. Our opinions are changing. Practitioners of cannabis can convince their patients that they are open to the possibilities that have been celebrated by patients during all of these years. We must accept the fact that we still know very little about THC and show patients that we are willing to uncover the many ways patients benefit from it. This will help restore our reputations as healers.

Trial and Error by Patients

Even if we make specific recommendations of THC doses, there will be a considerable amount of trial and error by patients. While they adjust to

---

[5] Statement of Dr. William C. Woodward. Legislative Council. American Medical Association. Druglibrary.org. http://www.druglibrary.org/Schaffer/hemp/taxact/woodward.htm Accessed: May 1, 2020.

using cannabis therapeutically, they will need to familiarize themselves with its effects and the high that it brings. Because of the range in concentrations and strengths of cannabis products, finding an optimal level of THC can be difficult so physicians should counsel patients to be careful and use as little as possible while they become accustomed to its effects.

This is a drug that has to be tapered to the individual, the condition being treated, and their *lifestyle*. A jazz musician will require a very different THC regimen than an airplane pilot. A young bachelor will medicate differently than a mother of five. The doses and effects of THC will change over time for individuals too. It is the job of the physician to form a close relationship with their patients so they can coach them on how to best treat their conditions given their individual circumstances and tolerance.

The general guidance we provide needs to be adjusted by patients on a day-to-day basis. Patients should be granted autonomy to self-manage their cannabis use. Physicians can provide them access to safer, legal THC products that have been tested and labeled for accurate dosing. However, THC is unlike traditional medications that have an exact dose to be taken at specific intervals. When it is inhaled, it is adjusted and titrated each time it is used. Because of this, the patients will need to judge for themselves how much to use and how often to take it. Thankfully, the medication is safe enough for patients to use this way, but we must always counsel them on safe practices.

Interdisciplinary Teamwork

It is advisable to always communicate plans of care with the patient's other healthcare providers. This will ensure safer management and provide an opportunity for interdisciplinary education. Teamwork will promote a culture among physicians that is receptive to medical advancements made possible with the use of THC.

As mentioned before, not all healthcare providers are accepting of medical cannabis. It is worth asking the patient how their other doctors would feel about discussing cannabis with you before they sign a consent for you to talk with those practitioners. If a patient feels uncomfortable notifying their other doctors of their medical cannabis use or believe their other doctor is against it, it may be wise to hold-off. Revisiting this at their follow-up appointments will be easier after a benefit from the THC treatment has been established. Using their progress as leverage for their continuation of cannabis will be helpful when breeching the subject with another physician who hasn't yet accepted cannabis as a legitimate form of medicine.

3 THE PATIENT ENCOUNTER

The information throughout this book, not just in this chapter, will be useful during patient encounters. Below are some important points that you should know when discussing cannabis with patients.

Initiation

The fastest way for physicians to gain their patients' trust is to begin by openly discussing their own use of cannabis. Even acknowledging that the physician has never used marijuana before but has learned about it in medical literature will establish trust with the patient. Otherwise, patients will spend much of the time of the encounter trying to figure out how much experience the physician has on the subject before appraising the worth of their recommendations. If the physician admits to never experiencing it personally but explains that they have a scientific understanding of it, patients will be interested to hear their professional viewpoint and will be captivated. Without knowing a physician's personal experience, however, patients may hold less value to the recommendations they receive.

Almost all patients have used marijuana at some point in their lives, regardless of if they admit to it or not. These patients do not need as much guidance from a physician but should be reminded of state-relevant laws and office protocols. Screen patients for legal problems and employment concerns since patients are sometimes encouraged by their parole officers to come in for a medical marijuana card appointment or they may have an impending urine drug screen for work. Such patients are there for reasons other than their own health and they seek a physician's services for sociopolitical reasons. These are still important reasons to help a patient. In the current political climate of America, it is too detrimental to the patient's long-term health and wellbeing to deny them the protection a marijuana card provides in a time of need. The opportunity to create a physician-patient relationship that provides medical guidance should not be wasted.

Marijuana-Naïve Patients

The experience of using marijuana for the first time is the most high-risk time for patients to overdose so marijuana-naïve patients require special attention and a significant amount of counseling. A typical encounter with an experienced patient requires only 15-20 minutes but a patient that has never used cannabis needs at least 30-45 minutes, sometimes longer. These cases need to be carefully counseled so it's important to identify them immediately. Up to half of patients say they have not used marijuana on their initial intake forms because they are afraid to admit that they have used it illegally. Physicians have to figure out which patients have truly never used it by asking the right questions during the patient encounter. Asking about their profession can occasionally provide insight into their experience. Doctors and police officers are a population that has not usually tried it before. For everyone else, an assessment of their social history will unveil their experience using cannabis.

One of the quickest ways to find out a patient's marijuana habits is to bluntly ask them if they "smoke weed." This may seem like coarse language, but it cuts straight to the heart of the matter. As mentioned earlier, the word weed is the most common non-medical term for marijuana and asking in this way will invite the patient to be open and honest about their use with you. It will relax them and demonstrate that you are hip to the subject. THC-naïve patients might be startled when asked this way and might appear slightly embarrassed for never having used marijuana. Asking if patients smoke weed is the best way to assess their comfort using marijuana.

Coaching First-Time Patients

Patients who have never used marijuana need extensive coaching and preparation. Their first experience feeling the effects of marijuana will be a trip. Instruct them to prepare a safe and comfortable environment. They can seek guidance from their relatives and friends, who have used marijuana. Having a caretaker to look over them is very valuable and most people are honored to be asked to help guide the patient as they become familiar with the effects. In the best situations, physicians can monitor first-time users during their induction, similar to how Suboxone® induction is monitored in physician offices. This is the safest way to introduce patients to the effects of cannabis.

Priming

For unknown reasons, the first administration of THC has no psychoactivity and serves to "prime" the patient for utilizing the medical benefit of cannabis. Sometimes patients don't inhale properly, and this delays the therapy until after proper systemic delivery is achieved. However, even in cases where the patient administers an effective dose, marijuana is not psychoactive until after an initial priming. Sometimes patients require multiple administrations on separate days to adequately prime them and to react to the medicine. Others don't need to be primed, possibly from a prior exposure, but this is uncommon.

Clinical Signs of Successful Inhalation
Exhaling before taking a puff.
Completing inhalation with fresh air to deliver all inhaled THC out of the pulmonary dead space and into the alveoli.
Deep thoracic cough following inhalation (not nasopharyngeal clearing).
Visible plume when exhaled.

To prime a patient, an oral dose of 10mg THC can be used, which is a substantial amount for a user that has not developed any tolerance. This is because we can expect that they will not have a response to the medicine until after this priming dose. After 24-48 hours, the endocannabinoid system adjusts, allowing THC to become physiologically active on the second administration. This is when the patient is most sensitive to its effects.

In the event that the patient responds to their first use (other than the common placebo effect), oral cannabis will last significantly longer and may be overwhelming. For this reason, inhaled cannabis is preferred in first time users, as it can be titrated more easily. The rapid onset of inhaled THC allows real-time monitoring. Using a high-quality pre-filled cartridge is the recommended inhalation method since it is less irritating and more controllable during administration than smoking. Instruct the patient that most vaporizers require five clicks to turn on and three to adjust their power level from low to medium to high. Each model is different, and they should ask their dispensary's budtender to instruct them on using the vape pen so they can start on the lowest setting. Warn the patient that the vapor is irritating to the airways and coughing is a normal adverse effect that diminishes with regular use.

Inhalation

Many first-time users do not inhale marijuana deep enough to the alveoli to adequately deliver THC to the body. Some of these patients believe that they have no response to the medicine and give up prematurely. Physicians can't depend on dispensary staff to teach patients and should take the time to coach first-time patients on how to inhale appropriately.

There are two ways to inhale marijuana. The first is directly to the lungs in a long continuous inhalation (a "drag"). This is more irritating to the upper airways because the vapor (or smoke) makes contact with the glottis and trachea for a longer period of time while it travels to the lower airways. The second method of inhalation is less irritating because it is done by forming a bolus of vapor that is then inhaled more rapidly in one shot. To do this, the vapor is "sipped" into the mouth, where the mucous membranes are less irritated by the presence of vapor or smoke. Only the mucous membranes of the respiratory system are sensitive during inhalation. Once the vapor is built up in the mouth, like sipping on a drink, fresh air can be inhaled so the bolus of vapor in the mouth is quickly sucked into the lungs and followed by fresh air. This is a less irritating way to inhale cannabis because it exposes the upper airways to the vapor for only a brief amount of time and the fresh air "chases" the bolus like water after a shot of alcohol.

When patients fail to inhale properly, it is usually from their fear of feeling pain and irritation in their lungs and throats. Inadequate delivery can manifest as hacking and snorting from coughing up vapor into their pharynx and nasal passageways. In contrast, a deep bronchial cough suggests that the vapor was adequately delivered into the lower airways and reached the alveoli. Encourage patients to chase each puff with fresh air so the vapor reaches these deeper areas of the lungs. This improves pulmonary delivery and systemic administration. Friends and family who can legally use marijuana should provide inspiration by demonstrating to the patient how to adequately inhale until the patient can do so on their own.

The First High

Once patients have primed themselves by successfully inhaling or ingesting marijuana, they can expect to feel the effects the following day when they try it again. We do not understand why THC requires priming for most people. No other pharmaceutical agent has this property. On the second successful attempt, the patient will feel the psychoactivity (the *high*) associated with cannabis use. A comfortable environment is conducive to psychological security and careful administration prevents negative experiences. Instruct patients to wait 10-15 minutes after each puff because there is a delayed response in first timers. This will prevent patients from overdosing and becoming paranoid. The side effects of cannabis are most pronounced in early users, so careful administration is especially important at this time. Sometimes there is no effect on the second day attempting marijuana, possibly because the first day's attempt did not deliver enough THC to the body to adequately prime the patient. The THC should work on the third day.

The first therapeutically active dose of THC has profound side-effects that are often parodied in popular culture. Characterizations of blood-shot eyes, the "munchies" and bouts of uncontrollable laughter really do happen to new users. Describing the psychoactive high of marijuana is difficult to explain in words and needs to be personally experienced to be completely understood. The feeling is more intense and surreal in new users than in chronic users, who become accustomed to the effect.

4 SIDE EFFECTS

Euphoria (aka feeling "High")

Being so lipophilic, THC distribution favors myelin-dense white-matter tracts interconnecting our brain's structural and functional components, resulting in a vague aura known as **"the high"**. The anatomically largest of these tracts is the corpus collosum, a myelin-rich structure connecting both hemispheres. When THC is deposited in the white matter of the corpus collosum of new users of cannabis, it results in a discrepancy relaying information between the hemispheres that creates ephemeral feelings of déjà vu and a seemingly lowered framerate of sensory input. The effect is like experiencing reality through a 1920's early film projector. This may be accompanied by protracted visual trailing of moving objects that is discontinuous, called an illusory palinopsia. For comparison, the *opposite* of this effect is experienced when watching high frame-rate HDTV that looks unrealistically smooth and feels artificial.

Side Effects of THC

Sensory Perception: Vibrant colors and trace visual hallucinations, Déjà vu (film projector effect), "tunnel vision" awareness, improved flavor and smell of food, enhanced timbre and rhythm of music, heightened sensitivity to tactile stimulation, protracted sense of time.

Psychological: (Neurocognition) Internal dialogue and introspection, critical self-reflection, short-term memory forgetfulness, increased inhibition and risk aversion, social awkwardness, discomfort of unfamiliar surroundings

(Emotional) Labile mood, laughter, embarrassment, anxiety, paranoia

Autonomic: (Sympathetic)- xerostomia and conjunctival injection, diaphoresis, tachycardia, palpitations

(Parasympathetic) – increased appetite (munchies), sleepiness, nausea (severe)

While high, there is a heightened sensory perception that results in greater appreciation of the surroundings. Perhaps because of the large myelin content of the olfactory bulbs, taste and smell is magnified, so food tastes better. Patients have short-term food cravings ("munchies") induced by hunger from CB1-activated ghrelin release.[6] Emotions are intensified, and mundane events can become humorous, evoking spouts of laughter. Alternatively, emotions can swing the other direction in the form of discomfort, anxiety and paranoia, especially at high THC doses and in new users. If the THC was consumed late in the day or at night, an inevitable sleepiness ensues.

The intensity of marijuana side effects is directly proportional to both the dose and the rate of intake of THC during administration. The fastest rate of ingestion is vaporizing concentrates at high temperature using an oil rig (dabbing). In extreme cases, a single inhalation can contain over a gram of THC. A rapid influx of THC into the body produces a catecholamine surge leading to palpitations, tachycardia and sometimes diaphoresis. Except in extremely high doses, these side effects are not usually present from oral administration of marijuana, which tends to be more tolerable because it takes longer to absorb.

Carefully inhaling small vaporized puffs of THC using a vape pen is the preferred route of administration for new users because it can be easily titrated and has just a two-hour duration. Consuming oral cannabis products can result in using too much because the rate of onset is close to two hours and the inexperienced user will be prone to taking additional doses while they wait for an effect. Unlike inhaled cannabis, if too much is taken, they will have to wait five hours before the side effects and the high dissipate.

Palpitations

Patients frequently experience palpitations following marijuana use, especially when inhaling and consuming a high dose of THC rapidly. Some patients are more prone to feeling palpitations, which can be unbearable for

---

[6] Mazidi, M, Taraghdari, SB, Rezaee, P. *et al.* The effect of hydroalcoholic extract of Cannabis Sativa on appetite hormone in rat. *J Complement Integr Med.* 2014;11(4):253-257. doi:10.1515/jcim-2014-0006.

them, limiting their ability to use the medicine. Palpitations can be eliminated by prescribing low-dose propranolol one hour before treatment similar to how it's used for anxiety-provoking events. This can be discontinued once the symptoms are tolerable.

> **THC-Induced Palpitation Rx:**
>
> Propranolol 10mg PO BID PRN one-hour before THC use.

Overdose

The side effects and likelihood of an adverse event diminish with repeated use but may return after a tolerance break. When too much is consumed, the cerebral effects can quickly overwhelm the unaccustomed user. Thankfully, THC overdoses are never fatal and always transient so instruct your patients not to worry if they are concerned of an overdose. Unless consumed orally, the effects will subside in two hours. The most common severe overdose leads to panic attacks.

Panic Attacks

Rarely, paranoia can lead to a severe panic attack. This frequently occurs when new patients misinterpret their initial THC priming as a subtherapeutic dose and then proceed to overcompensate on their second attempt. In my experience with patients, I have discovered an effective management that has – so far – proved reliable and safe. First, let me explain the mechanism by which a marijuana-related panic attack occurs so you understand the reasoning for my seemingly unorthodox approach.

Inexperienced patients can become paranoid that they have used too much and are experiencing an adverse reaction. THC's positive inotropy produces palpitations that reinforce the patient's suspicions of a life-threatening event. Panic ensues and the patient attempts to maintain control by conscious breathing techniques, despite normal oxygenation.

Hyperventilation expels carbon dioxide and increases serum alkalinity, which triggers vasoconstriction in the brain. These vascular adjustments in the brain's blood flow are sensed as a dyspnea that persists after a deep breath. Another breath is attempted and then a cascade of hyperventilation attempts, each time failing to deliver a satisfactory breath leading to presyncope. By this point, the patient is afraid of impending death and seeks emergent care.

To short-circuit this psychogenic downward spiral, the patient can reverse the process by briefly *holding* their breath to build up carbon dioxide and restore a hemodynamic state capable of inciting respiratory satisfaction. Afterwards, patients will have psychological closure from the feeling of adequately "catching their breath" that occurs when ventilation-induced vasoconstriction restores vascular resistance to their hypercapnic, vasodilated states. Eliminating dyspnea this way is not possible when already vasoconstricted from hyperventilation-induced alkalosis during a panic attack.

Repeated Use

The adverse effects of THC diminish with repeated use. Side effects, like palpitations or paranoia, typically resolve after 6-8 weeks while the therapeutic properties of marijuana are retained. This makes THC an unusual medication whose therapeutic window widens with increased use. Other drugs are the opposite: the more they are used, the higher the risk of side effects and overdose while their therapeutic benefit often diminishes. THC, on the other hand, is better appreciated by chronic users because the side effects become tolerable and the benefits become more evident, especially at higher doses. The tolerance is irregularly selective for unwanted adverse-effects and resistant to primary effects.[7]

Severe Conditions and Consequences

I have never witnessed the rare but serious adverse effects of THC reported in the literature. After years in this specialty, a single case of THC-induced psychosis, cannabis hyperemesis syndrome, or inhalation-pneumothorax would be a statistical coincidence rather than a direct cause of cannabis treatment, were it to occur in one of my patients. Out of thousands

---

[7] Pertwee, RG. The diverse CB1 and CB2 receptor pharmacology of three plant cannabinoids: delta9-tetrahydrocannabinol, cannabidiol and delta9-tetrahydrocannabivarin. *Br J Clin Pharmacol.* 2008;153(2):199–215. doi:10.1038/sj.bjp.0707442.

of patients that I have approved for medical marijuana treatment, only one of them was suspicious of cannabis-induced psychosis.

None of my patients has suffered e-cigarette vaporization associated lung injury (EVALI), also known as vaping-associated pulmonary injury (VAPI). In fact, approving patients for medical marijuana may have prevented cases because EVALI has been associated with black-market products containing vitamin E acetate[8][9] so providing access to state-approved dispensaries protects patients from that risk. State-approved dispensaries test their products to assure safety.

By far, the most severe consequences to patients are sociopolitical. Employment drug screens, disapproving family members, DUIs, and criminal convictions are too frequently an outcome of marijuana use. Thankfully, these can be diminished in patients who are counseled on proper methods to use and helped certified for legal (state) use for therapeutic purposes. Tell patients to keep their cannabis use confidential, the way pain killers and benzodiazepines would be.

---

[8] Centers for Disease Control and Prevention. Outbreak of Lung Injury Associated with the Use of E-Cigarette, or Vaping, Products. Centers for Disease Control and Prevention. https://www.cdc.gov/tobacco/basic_information/e-cigarettes/severe-lung-disease.html. Accessed: May 1. 2020.

[9] Blount, BC, Karwowski, MP, Shields, PG. *et al.* Vitamin E acetate in bronchoalveolar-lavage fluid associated with EVALI. *N Engl J Med.* 2020;382(8):697-705. doi:10.1056/NEJMoa1916433.

5 DOSE AND TYPES

Inhaled THC doses cannot be practically measured in milligrams for a number of reasons. Foremost, the products on the market vary in potency. Flower varies from hemp or CBD-only strains containing less than 0.3% THC that can be sold over the counter to strains containing 30% or higher THC. The concentration of THC in flower varies from plant to plant and even depends on the location on the stalk it is picked from. Marijuana increases in strength the higher it is picked on the stalk. Concentrates range from 50% THC to as high as 100% THC. Pre-filled vape pens can vary from CBD-only products to 90% or higher THC. The second reason it impossible to measure the exact dose of inhaled marijuana is because the duration of an inhalation is not standardized. Some patients can take a tiny puff, others a long drag, or multiple puffs in sequence.

Inform patients that products with higher concentrations of THC can deliver equivalent doses with less vapor and smaller puffs. The volume of vapor inhaled varies depending on frequency of use and user preferences. New users will quickly feel pulmonary irritation upon inhalation and will cough, expelling the vapor before a significant amount of lung volume is filled. If the volume inhaled is less than the dead space in their airways, no systemic delivery will take place because the vapor won't reach the alveoli. Instead, the vapor stays in the upper airways where no gas exchange occurs. Sometimes patients will give up trying because each time they inhale this way, they fail to have an effect. Experienced users prevent this by chasing their puffs with fresh air to ensure all inhaled THC reaches the terminal airways.

After patients grow accustomed to inhaling marijuana, they can adjust the dose of THC to fit their needs and preferences by changing the size and strength of their inhalations. For example, a series of small puffs can more comfortably deliver the same dose of THC over time than one long drag can. On the other hand, a long drag can instantly deliver the same dose as many smaller puffs but will be difficult to tolerate in unaccustomed users.

The Dr. Roman Globe Method[10]

Using a reasonably-priced vaporizer for marijuana concentrates, I have devised a volume-dosed administration technique that delivers a consistent *volume* of THC vapor to protect first-time patients from using too much. The dose of THC will slightly change depending on the concentration of THC in the concentrate used but it will at least allow for a consistent amount between puffs. It is also less irritating to the airways and improves chances of a successful inhalation. I recommend advising patients of this technique if they are new to using marijuana and if they are interested in trying concentrates for their first time.

The technique uses a vaporizer pen with a clear chamber on top. The chamber is made of glass so patients can see how much vapor is inside of it. In the middle of the glass "globe" chamber, there is an atomizer that a small amount of concentrate can be placed on, approximately the size of a grain of rice. When the vape pen is activated, the atomizer vaporizes the concentrate into vapor that has a higher density than room air. The vapor fills the chamber and displaces the air above it, creating a visible level that increases from the bottom to the top as the chamber fills. Patients can click the vape pen to activate the vaporization process until the vapor reaches a consistent volume inside the chamber before inhaling it.

Instruct first-time users to pre-fill the chamber with vapor until it is half-full (app. 1mL in vapor volume). Then, they can release the battery button so that vaporization stops and inhale the contents of the chamber until its visibly cleared. This allows a consistent dose of THC to be inhaled with each puff. Patients can anticipate more accurately how high they will become and how much to use to treat their condition.

Dose Adjustments from Oral to Inhaled

Once a patient is familiar with the effects of inhaled THC, they can try it by mouth. Oral cannabis products can be dosed more accurately when they are properly tested by dispensaries and marijuana manufacturers for

---

[10] Email info@natureswaymedicine.com for information on purchasing such pens for your clinic.

their THC contents and appropriately labeled. However, food infused with THC, called *edibles* may be very high in THC potency. There are edibles with many hundreds of milligrams of THC infused in them. Because of this, edible marijuana products are the most common cause of THC-related emergency room visits.[11] Instruct patients to be very cautious when ordering medical marijuana edibles and to start with small pieces of them, waiting a couple hours, and trying again, if more is necessary. If patients find benefit from oral THC, specific milligram doses can be recommended, unlike inhaled products. Since the rate of onset after oral consumption is two hours, the marijuana should be consumed as early in the day as possible, assuming no driving or mentally-taxing responsibilities will need to take place while the patient is high.

We can use dronabinol (Marinol®) as a reliable reference point for THC dosing because its active ingredient is also THC and it has used FDA pharmaceutical-grade testing during manufacturing. The lowest dose of dronabinol is 2.5mg per pill, which in my experience is therapeutically insufficient for patients using dispensary marijuana products. The reality is that patients consume products made by sub-pharmaceutical grade manufacturers with financial incentives to overstate THC content. While the testing and labeling of dispensary products is better than those on the black-market, there is still more room for error than with pharmaceutical drugs like dronabinol.

When I began treating patients with medical marijuana, it was with dronabinol in hospitals. Patients were ordered 5mg PO dronabinol off-label for cachexia and failure to thrive in the ICU. This was an important part of my career as a physician because I witnessed the beneficial effects of THC in these patients. Later, those patient interactions would inspire me to begin my full-time career in marijuana medicine. Once I started recommending marijuana to patients who would purchase from dispensaries, I realized that THC products are sold in higher doses at dispensaries. In time, I found a safe starting dose that was significantly higher than dronabinol capsules but

---

[11] Monte AA, Shelton SK, Mills E. *et al.* Acute Illness Associated with Cannabis Use, by Route of Exposure: An Observational Study. *Ann Intern Med.* 2019;170:531–537. [Epub ahead of print 26 March 2019]. doi:10.7326/M18-2809.

relatively low compared to most oral marijuana products.

The starting oral dose of THC that I recommend to my medical marijuana patients purchasing products from state-run dispensaries is **12.5mg**. Many products can be broken into increments of 12.5, such as 100mg square gummies cut into eighths. Unless otherwise specified, when I refer to a low dose of oral THC, I specifically mean 12.5mg, which has proven to be both reliable and safe in my patients. As patients become accustomed to the euphoric high experienced from the medicine, they can increase the dose, but 12.5 mg is a safe starting point for marijuana newcomers. Experienced users can take over one hundred milligrams of THC per dose.

Sometimes patients mistake THCA for THC. Counsel your patients to check that their oral marijuana products contain THC instead of THCA, the inactive precursor present in raw flower that decarboxylates into THC at high temperatures when baked, vaporized or ignited. If the products contain THCA, there will be no physiological effect from the medication after oral ingestion.

If patients can't accurately measure a 12.5mg dose of THC, instruct them to gradually titrate an incremental dose of their oral cannabis product on subsequent days until they begin to feel the effects. Presence of at least some psychoactivity ensures an acceptable level was administered. If a patient gets too high, the dose can be lowered on subsequent administrations. If the patient does not feel psychoactivity, they may be using a subtherapeutic dose that is ineffective for physiological activity. Depending on the condition being treated, patients can be encouraged to develop a tolerance to the side-effect of feeling slightly high rather than lowering the dose too much. In some situations, as will be discussed later, patients *should* feel moderately to severely high in order to treat their condition successfully. However, the low dose of 12.5mg will not cause patients to reach this kind of level of euphoria, only a mild high usually.

Users who bake marijuana into food and make "edibles" on their own take the risk of over-medicating or spoiling their cannabis. They should be warned to be very careful since there is always trial and error when preparing and consuming marijuana this way. The dose administered is inaccurate because the calculations to determine the THC content in milligrams are misleading and based on ideal conditions far different from patient kitchens. Also, the THC is usually derived from marijuana flower, which we know varies in potency.

Cooking Marijuana Butter

The usual method of cooking marijuana is by grinding it finely and adding it to melted butter on the stove at low heat. Approximately one ounce of marijuana can be used for one pound of butter. Cooking it for a couple hours decarboxylates the THCA into THC. The butter should be strained to remove the flower. I recommend to my patients that they pour the remaining butter into ice-cube trays and store it in the freezer. Once it hardens, it can be used like regular butter for recipes. Most commonly, the butter will be used for baking cookies or brownies. The same process can be done with oil on the stove and the oil can also be used in recipes or for salad dressing, as an example. Food prepared this way is often described as being "infused" with cannabis or THC. As mentioned, accurate THC dosing this way is very difficult so infusing food to treat conditions is safest for patients who have developed a high tolerance, so they have a lower chance of an overdose.

Microdosing	Macrodosing
Minor depression, stress, minor aches and pains, IBS	Migraines, PTSD, cancer, acute severe pain, acute anxiety

Microdosing

Microdosing is the use of THC in small amounts often on an as-needed basis. The patient will be barely high, almost not at all. The purpose is to stimulate homeostasis maintenance and relieve stress on the body and mind. This method of medicating is optimal for healthier patients with milder conditions. Microdosing relieves acute psychological stress,[12] chronic aches and pains,[13] and may slow the accumulation of microcellular damage due to

---

[12] Micale V, Drago F. Endocannabinoid system, stress and HPA axis. *Eur J Pharmacol.* 2018;834:230-239. doi:10.1016/j.ejphar.2018.07.039.

[13] Abraham AD, Leung EJY, Wong BA. *et al.* "Orally consumed cannabinoids provide

THE CLINICIAN'S GUIDE TO MEDICAL CANNABIS

the anti-inflammatory properties of THC.[14] Theoretically, this could slow the inevitable natural processes that lead to aging.[15] One day THC may prove beneficial for maintaining long-term optimal health. It certainly has not been shown to be significantly detrimental in chronic users, even at high doses.

Macrodosing

Macrodosing is use of THC in doses that produce a strong high. This is often done at the end of the day when the mind can rest assured that the day's responsibilities are completed. It can abort acute conditions like migraines or autoimmune flares and protects from triggers of post-traumatic stress disorder. Acute psychological conditions like a bout of anxiety are treated this way to restore the mind to baseline and break mental feedback loops gone awry, like self-perpetuating negative thoughts. For some people, macrodosing is the best way to rest at the end of the day and prevents burn out from stressful and demanding lifestyles.

Making Recommendations for Patients

Recommendations should be made in conjunction with the patient and are based on the individual's medical condition but adapted to their lifestyle. The physician's responsibility is to guide the patient so they can find the most effective treatment that conforms to their way of life. This requires consideration of their morals, families, employment responsibilities, out-of-state travel, and other socioeconomic factors.

Many patients have difficulty affording enough cannabis to optimally treat their conditions. Hopefully, U.S. citizens will be allowed to grow cannabis themselves soon for free, like in Canada. For some, this will be a gateway out of the American healthcare crisis. In the meantime, patients are usually overcharged hyperinflated prices by state-approved dispensaries or

---

long-lasting relief of allodynia in a mouse model of chronic neuropathic pain". *Neuropsychopharmacol.* 2019. doi:10.1038/s41386-019-0585-3

[14] Beydogan AB, Coskun ZMm Bolkent, S. The protective effects of Δ9-tetrahydrocannabinol against inflammation and oxidative stress in rat liver with fructose-induced hyperinsulinemia. *J Pharm Pharmacol.* 2019;71:408-416. doi:10.1111/jphp.13042.

[15] Sarne Y. Beneficial and deleterious effects of cannabinoids in the brain: the case of ultra-low dose THC. *Am J Drug Alcohol Abuse.* 2019;45(6):551-562. doi:10.1080/00952990.2019.1578366.

black-market dealers. Costs are too high for many patients that need daily treatment, especially once tolerance develops. Insurance does not cover the price of marijuana like other drugs so physicians should prioritize the value of care by maximizing the amount of THC available to use.

THC percentage

Marijuana prices are categorized according to its form, with little variation between manufacturers or potency. For example, the price of concentrates containing 60% THC and 90% THC will be relatively the same. Also, products containing CBD are priced the same as their THC counterparts, even though CBD has no physiological effect in the body. A cartridge with oil containing CBD marketed at a 1:1 ratio will cost the same as a THC-only cartridge but will contain half as much active ingredient because the THC is effectively diluted. Inhaling more vapor to deliver the same dose of THC consumes cartridges quicker so tell patients to purchase products with the most THC because they require less inhalation to treat their conditions and are more affordable.

In most cases, cannabis oil is sold by weight, for example in milligrams per oral capsule or in 250mg, 500mg and 1-gram cartridges for vaporization. Capsules are usually dosed by milligrams of THC but concentrates and cartridges are sold by weight of total product, including non-physiologically active constituents (terpenes, CBD, byproducts, etc.). This is why the percentage of THC is so important when determining which products to use.

Occasionally, cannabis oil is sold by volume in syringes for less cost (per milligram THC) than if it were sold by weight. In such products, the percentage of THC is calculated as a percentage of weight using mass spectroscopy but then sold by volume of oil. These syringes are filled with oil to a specified volume but are sometimes priced like products sold by weight. Since THC-containing oil has a density of about 2 grams THC per milliliter, a one milliliter volume syringe contains about twice as much THC as one gram of concentrate sold by weight. So, if a milliliter of THC-oil costs as much as a gram of THC concentrate, purchasing the milliliter of oil is more cost-effective and about half as expensive per milligram of THC.

Types of Strains

One of the most asked questions is what type of strain to use for a specific condition. The most often perpetuated myth about marijuana purports that there are strains better suited for certain conditions. According to this theory, there exist two main strains called *Indica* and *Sativa*, which behave like downers and uppers, respectively. In reality, all strains are hybrids of the two, with few differences between them and relative phenotypical uniformity. We have not cultivated marijuana into distinct varieties like we have with apple cultivars. The differences between Indica and Sativa are an artifact of the placebo effect. When patients are told that they will feel a certain way after using a particular strain, there is a confirmation bias effect that occurs, and patients believe that they are feeling the way they expected from the strain they purchased.

There is no "entourage effect" from strain-specific substances. The most revered strains are simply those that contain the most THCA. If terpenes present in the strain were responsible for medical properties, we would already know this in the scientific literature since these terpenes are not schedule 1 substances and would have been studied thoroughly by now. Explaining this to your patients helps them more effectively choose products independently, relying less on dispensary staff.

6 DISPENSARIES AND INPATIENTS

Dispensary Staff Members

There are two types of staff members at dispensaries that help patients choose products: pharmacists and "budtenders." Due to the lack of research available about marijuana, both pharmacists and budtenders are influenced by pseudoscience and the industry's market trends. That is why it is important to coach your patients before they go to the dispensaries. Dispensary staff will often make claims that have no scientific standing. For example, they will claim that some products are better for the day and others at night. This is misleading as both products contain the same active ingredients (THC & THCA). In the worst cases, dispensary staff members will have financial incentives to sell higher-priced or slow-selling products that wiser patients know not to buy.

Tell your patients to be skeptical at dispensaries and to take what is said to them with a grain of salt. Remind them not to waste money on CBD or terpenes, which drive prices up and contain less THC or THCA. Advise patients to purchase products with the most THC and THCA for the cheapest price. For example, a strain of marijuana with 25% THC that costs the same as a strain with 20% THC is more value for the money and less needs to be administered to reach the same effect.

Having said that, dispensary staff can be helpful instructing patients on *how to use* marijuana products. New patients can get confused with the variety of vaporizers and other products on the market. Budtenders will advise the patients on how to use cartridges and concentrates. The quality of the instructions will vary from state to state depending on their restrictions and laws. For example, in Pennsylvania dispensaries are not allowed to unpack products to show patients, so staff can only describe products to patients without physically showing them.

Forming Ties with Dispensaries

Communication with dispensaries is very important for some cases.

In most states that have legalized medical marijuana, physicians are barred from conducting business with dispensaries to prevent referral kickbacks and unfair market advantages. Having worked with dispensaries in two states, I have seen greatly different attitudes towards comanaging patients. Dispensary cooperation is hit-or-miss. I have seen adverse events from poor dispensary recommendations to patients that would have been prevented if I were notified of the changes. In contrast, some of the best treatment results have come from close communication between me and the dispensary pharmacist.

I encourage developing strong ties with local dispensaries so that they are receptive to your recommendations when the need arises. If the relationship is strong enough, they can develop a sense of which products you prefer your patients to use and adjust their recommendations accordingly.

Communication with the dispensary is especially important for pediatric patients and patients unable to make decisions for themselves. Children receiving marijuana have to be careful about how much they use and there needs to be close planning between the parents, dispensary staff and yourself. If they use a vape pen at school, even legally, there can be significant consequences. At the very least, other students will gossip about it and at worst, a school may not tolerate this medication on its premises and expel the student.

Nursing Home Patients

One of the most complicated situations occurs when treating patients who live in a skilled nursing facility (SNF) and those residing in an assisted living facility (ALF). These facilities have protocols for dispensing controlled substances to prevent diversion, but they are not easily adhered to with marijuana products.

Typically, the protocols require clearly labeled containers that display the medication's name, form, route of administration, dose in milligrams and frequency of use. Marijuana products can be difficult to describe this way. Inhaled products are usually one to two puffs every two hours as needed (Q2H PRN). Oral products are usually easier to provide instructions for when in a capsule form, but the other forms of oral cannabis are less simple.

It is very useful to consult with the pharmacist at the patient's dispensary when coming up with instructions to provide the SNF/ALF.

Marijuana products at dispensaries vary from month to month and often lack consistency. Companies sell strains chosen for each growing cycle so when patients need to fill up on their medicine, there may be completely different strains available than the previous ones they were using. This makes it hard to provide patients at SNFs and ALFs consistent instructions on what to use. Discussing products with dispensary pharmacists can help determine which products will be available over many months and which are going to run out and never return. Pick a product that a patient's facility can become familiar with. It is already a big step for these facilities to approve cannabis treatment without the added confusion of changing products from month to month and requiring new instructions for each one.

Facilities usually place instruction labels on marijuana products while they are stored so that nurses know clearly how and when to treat patients. When products change, new labels must be written, and facilities need to communicate with the physician recommending the products to know what to put on the new labels. Sometimes, the dispensaries are the ones that put the labels on the products before providing them to the patient or their facility. In these circumstances, the dispensary may have to speak to you, the patient's doctor, before supplying the instructions for the labels. Usually, it is most practical to approve and specify administration instructions for products chosen by the patient or their caretakers while they were at the dispensary. Administering medication for patients at SNF/ALF facilities is definitely a team effort due to the technicalities involved. When medical marijuana is finally descheduled and a federally approved treatment, it will be prescribed like other medications to patients but, in the meantime, it requires cooperation between the nursing home, patient or their caretaker, the dispensary pharmacist, and the physician making the recommendations.

Hospitalized Patients

Marijuana may be useful in patients who are hospitalized. Problems with over-sedation and overprescribing of opioids for pain could be mitigated with the use of marijuana on inpatients. Unfortunately, I have not had much experience with patients who are treated with cannabis in hospitals. Only once was I told that a patient was allowed to use cannabis products while hospitalized. It is uncertain to me if this was done officially by the attending physicians or if this was "under the table" treatment allowed by tertiary staff.

What I recommend to my patients who require inpatient treatment is to disclose their medical cannabis use to their hospital physicians and request dronabinol as an off-label replacement. This has been done successfully by a handful of my patients and the dronabinol helped control their symptoms. Since dronabinol is generally a very low-dosed THC capsule (2.5mg, 5mg & 10mg capsules), patients should request the highest doses that attending physicians will feel comfortable ordering for them. Pharmaceutical THC in the form of dronabinol has the same effects as medical marijuana THC so it can be very helpful for patients to continue this and it may be useful in post-surgical pain control, improving appetite and hospital-induced insomnia, among other symptoms. One recent study showed decreased hospital stay in patients who use marijuana following spinal fusion surgery.[16]

[16] Jakoi AM, Kirchner GJ, Kerbel YE, Iorio JA, Khalsa AS. The Effects of Marijuana Use on Lumbar Spinal Fusion. *Spine* (Phila Pa 1976). 2019 Nov 15. doi:10.1097/BRS.0000000000003321. [Epub ahead of print] PubMed PMID: 31770339.

7 PRIMARY CARE

Lifestyle Change Encouragement

Starting patients on medical marijuana provides a wonderful opportunity for encouraging lifestyle transformation. As physicians, our most difficult task is to change a patient's daily routines to improve their long-term health. We can use marijuana to leverage behavioral changes in our patients that would otherwise be too difficult.

Physical Activity

The first way you can influence your patient's lifestyle is to anchor cannabis treatment to physical activity. Exercise is beneficial for both physical and mental health so combining it with marijuana improves patient outcomes. Safety is important when exercising high so counsel patients to use small amounts of marijuana and not lift heavy weights. Light exercise, like walking, jogging and yoga are a good start for patients using marijuana. I recommend to my patients that they use marijuana before such activities on a daily basis to improve their overall outcome. In my experience, medical marijuana treats anxiety and pain more effectively when combined with physical activity. Tell your patients this so they exercise after using it. When patients take this advice, they receive the beneficial properties of THC while becoming more physically active. This has a positive result on their weight loss, strength, and overall wellbeing. One study has even shown that tetrahydrocannabinol use is associated with a small but statistically significant increase in testosterone.[17]

Weight Loss & Dieting

While traditionally marijuana is associated with appetite stimulation, I have found that in chronic users it can suppress appetite as well. The

---

[17] Fantus RJ, Lokeshwar SD, Kohn TP, Ramasamy R. The effect of tetrahydrocannabinol on testosterone among men in the United States: results from the National Health and Nutrition Examination Survey. *World J Urol.* 2020 Feb 17. doi: 10.1007/s00345-020-03110-5. [Epub ahead of print] PubMed PMID: 32067074.

endocannabinoid system is known to be involved in appetite regulation. Patients who are new to marijuana will undoubtedly have acute increases in appetite (*munchies*) when they use it. However, in my chronic patients I typically see weight loss instead of weight gain, which is uncommon in typical patients in a family medicine setting. Most people gain weight over time unless they actively try to lose weight, yet in my marijuana patients I see the opposite is true even without a change in physical activity. It appears that chronic marijuana use lowers appetite. If we remind ourselves that THC stimulates homeostasis in the body, this makes perfect sense. Our society today causes obesity from over-snacking and increased appetite and food consumption. THC suppresses this unnatural hyperactivity of our appetite and brings it back to normal.

Once a patient develops enough tolerance to the munchies, they can use marijuana as a substitute for snacking. Obese patients can replace snacks with a small puff to alleviate food cravings between meals. Let patients know that they should take a small inhaled dose of marijuana when they instead would reach for a snack between meals. This can suppress their craving and regulate a normal two-to-three meal per day diet without snack consumption between the meals.

Marijuana has been associated with lower body mass index (BMI)[181920] and counseling patients in creative ways provides clinicians new tools for long-term weight loss in patients and possibly secondary

---

[18] Giorgi V, Bongiovanni S, Atzeni F, Marotto D, Salaffi F, Sarzi-Puttini P. Adding medical cannabis to standard analgesic treatment for fibromyalgia: a prospective observational study. *Clin Exp Rheumatol.* 2020 Jan-Feb;38 Suppl. 123(1):53-59. Epub: 2020 Feb 5. PubMed PMID: 32116208.

[19] Alshaarawy O, Anthony JC. Are cannabis users less likely to gain weight? Results from a national 3-year prospective study. *Int J Epidemiol.* 2019 Oct 1;48(5):1695-1700. doi:10.1093/ije/dyz044. PubMed PMID: 30879064; PubMed Central PMCID: PMC6857742.

[20] Le Strat Y, Le Foll B. Obesity and cannabis use: results from 2 representative national surveys. *Am J Epidemiol.* 2011 Oct 15;174(8):929-33. doi: 10.1093/aje/kwr200. Epub: 2011 Aug 24. PubMed PMID: 21868374.

improvements in their glycemic control[21][22] and hypertension.[23] Epidemiological studies have shown that marijuana users have significantly less diabetes, hyperlipidemia and hypertension. Recommending that patients use medical marijuana as a substitute for snacks and in combination with physical therapy are a great way to take advantage of these potential effects of THC.

Insomnia

One of the best functions of cannabis is to maintain a healthy sleep cycle. Some of the earliest studies of cannabis proved its ability to induce sleep even in an uncomfortable environment. In the 1970's it was discovered that mice could keep balance on a wire but would stress out trying to stay on it. Eventually, the mice would fall off from exhaustion. Cannabis had a wonderful effect on these mice. When administered THC, mice were able to fall asleep on the wire. This test was dubbed the "ring test" and proved that marijuana was able to help sleep even in a state of psychological and physical stress.[24] Not surprisingly, CBD had no effect.

THC induces sleepiness without subduing the consciousness as a whole, the way other medications do. Most medications that are used for insomnia function on the GABA receptor and create an overall cognitive decline and lethargy. Marijuana causes an initial euphoria but the sleep it induces lasts longer than the high does. In today's society, people are constantly in front of phones, television screens or computers. Patients' sleep cycles shift into the night and the normal timing of sleep is disrupted. The

[21] Ngueta G, Ndjaboue R. Lifetime marijuana use in relation to insulin resistance in lean, overweight, and obese US adults. *J Diabetes.* 2020 Jan;*12*(1):38-47. doi:10.1111/1753-0407.12958. Epub: 2019 Jul 1. PubMed PMID: 31152633.

[22] Palomares B, Ruiz-Pino F, Garrido-Rodriguez M. *et al.* Tetrahydrocannabinolic acid A (THCA-A) reduces adiposity and prevents metabolic disease caused by diet-induced obesity. *Biochem Pharmacol.* 2020 Jan;171:113693. doi:10.1016/j.bcp.2019.113693. Epub: 2019 Nov 9. PubMed PMID: 31706843.

[23] Parekh T, Pemmasani S, Desai R. Marijuana Use Among Young Adults (18-44 Years of Age) and Risk of Stroke: A Behavioral Risk Factor Surveillance System Survey Analysis. *Stroke.* 2020 Jan;51(1):308-310. doi:10.1161/STROKEAHA.119.027828. Epub: 2019 Nov 11. PubMed PMID: 31707926.

[24] Pertwee RG. The ring test: a quantitative method for assessing the 'cataleptic' effect of cannabis in mice. *Br J Pharmacol.* 1972 Dec;46(4):753-63. doi:10.1111/j.1476-5381.1972.tb06900.x. PubMed PMID: 4655271; PubMed Central PMCID: PMC1666359.

homeostasis-regulating properties of THC affect sleep as well. Patients who feel restless at night and have trouble falling asleep can be treated with THC to bring themselves back to a natural sleep cycle.

When THC is consumed at night, patients become sleepy towards the end of the high. Actually, the medicine can have a stimulating effect right after it is used and can prevent sleep if taken too soon before bed. The high is excitatory in the beginning. Towards the end of the high is when the patient becomes sleepy and the brain more tired. Recommend to your patients that they use marijuana approximately two hours before bedtime. If they take it right before bed, they will have trouble falling asleep. Once the high is fading away, they will become tired in a natural way. Closing their eyes and laying their head down on a pillow will trigger their sleep, instead of forcing sleep with lethargy that is induced by drugs like benzodiazepines or zolpidem.

Alcohol and Tobacco

Many patients use alcohol as an escape mechanism to relax at the end of the day or to help them go to sleep. The health consequences of using alcohol are obvious and lowering alcohol consumption in patients is an important part of primary care. Substituting alcohol with marijuana is an effective way to lower alcohol use in patients. This will have beneficial secondary effects on their blood pressure, sleep, and protect them from a possible DUI (though make sure to inform patients not to drive while high, especially while they are new to the medicine). Many of my patients have managed to quit alcohol completely by using marijuana instead.

The same can be done for tobacco. We should remind ourselves how many deaths are attributed to alcohol and tobacco use and the lives we would save if those people were using cannabis instead. No one has died from cannabis.

Polypharmacy Consolidation

Medical marijuana is helpful for multiple conditions. As a homeostasis regulator, it affects multiple organ systems. Today's medical environment often leads patients to be on many medications to treat a variety of underlying conditions. This is unsafe and associated with decreased quality of life, mobility and cognition.[25]

Cannabis can be a gateway out of medication dependency and polypharmacy by serving as a replacement for multiple medications. Consolidating medications into THC treatment can be a wonderful way to improve patient quality of life and make it easier for them to manage their conditions themselves.

For example, a patient on SSRIs, gabapentin for neuropathy, zolpidem for insomnia, NSAIDs and tramadol for chronic pain would be a good candidate for cannabis treatment. By starting cannabis and recommending that it be used in combination with physical activity, you can tell the patient that it should treat their underlying conditions in a way that allows removing the other medications. Explain the risks of tramadol and that it causes dependency. Tell the patient that marijuana will improve the patient's mood and that SSRIs may not be necessary after starting marijuana. Instruct the patient to take a puff of inhaled THC as needed for chronic pain and neuropathy. You may find that the patient begins to come off of many of the medications used to treat their symptoms. Patients will appreciate you for this and will be amazed at the wonderful way that cannabis works. I have seen these results in many patients. Make sure to tell them that certain medications should stay, like blood pressure and diabetes medications. However, by combining marijuana treatment with exercise, even those may not be needed after a while.

In most states, marijuana cards need to be renewed annually. Explain to the patient your expectations for renewing their card and the need to consolidate polypharmacy: If the purpose of cannabis treatment is pain relief, remaining on the same doses of opiates after starting cannabis suggests a lack of benefit and does not warrant continuation of marijuana at their renewal appointment. Provide similar encouragement for eliminating anxiolytics, like benzodiazepines, hypnotics for insomnia and other medications wherever possible. This will provide an added pressure on the patient to discontinue unnecessary addictive medications. They will have an incentive to discontinue

---

[25] Maher RL, Hanlon J, Hajjar ER. Clinical consequences of polypharmacy in elderly. *Expert Opin Drug Saf.* 2014;13(1):57–65. doi:10.1517/14740338.2013.827660.

more dangerous drugs if they want to continue marijuana treatment.

8 PAIN MANAGEMENT

Most patients seeking marijuana suffer from chronic pain, which can be psychogenic, inflammatory, neuropathic, or a combination. They often exaggerate their symptoms to persuade your approval for a marijuana card and it can be difficult to assess their pain accurately. In spite of this, maintaining a low threshold for marijuana treatment is sound considering its safety relative to opiates and long-term use of NSAIDs. Physicians should never be criticized for liberally providing patients this alternative.

How Marijuana Relieves Pain

Unlike traditional neurotransmitters, THC functions on *pre*synaptic receptors (CB1 receptors). These receptors are coupled to Gi proteins that lower cAMP levels and shorten the duration of presynaptic action potentials. They also prevent calcium entry into the cell, a requirement for vesicle release, decreasing the transmitter that enters the synapse upon release. These two inhibitory mechanisms play a function in desensitizing pain stimulation in the spinal cord.

THC effects the dorsal horn in the spine at interneuronal connections that control our perception of pain by modifying the intensity of the signals relayed to the brain. These accommodation pathways sensitize or desensitize us to afferent stimulation responsible for the pathology underlying chronic pain. Unlike opiates, which block pain receptors and create dependency through receptor upregulation, THC modifies the spine's signaling pathways to improve tolerability of pain rather than the actual intensity of the signaling of peripheral pain receptors.[26] This improved tolerability allows patients to refocus their attention on other things.

---

[26] Pertwee RG. The diverse CB1 and CB2 receptor pharmacology of three plant cannabinoids: delta9-tetrahydrocannabinol, cannabidiol and delta9-tetrahydrocannabivarin. *Br J Pharmacol.* 2008;153(2):199–215. doi:10.1038/sj.bjp.0707442.

THC's second mechanism of pain relief is its anti-inflammatory properties following activation of CB2 receptors on the immune system's pro-inflammatory cells.[27] Binding to this receptor causes THC to inhibit activity and cytokine-mediated recruitment of lymphocytes. Autoimmune conditions and age-related osteoarthritic inflammation improve at baseline and during flare-ups, slowing long-term disease progression.

Topical treatment

Superficial and peripheral inflammatory pain can be treated with topical THC first. The treatment has only a local effect and is optimal for patients that don't want to feel high. I have had entire families and groups of friends seek marijuana cards to have access to topical THC products. Applying two to three times daily to the affected area provides significant relief from the anti-inflammatory properties of THC. Penetration to the joints of the periphery is variable and deep conditions like spinal degenerative disc disease are less amenable to topical therapy.

THC Pain Ladder

Topical

Inhaled PRN

Oral BID

Titrate Doses Up

Systemic administration of THC can also be attempted as an alternative or adjunct to topical treatment. Creams are not always available so patients should be familiar with other forms of use. Pain that persists despite application of topical THC warrants escalation of therapy to systemic forms.

First, vaporized THC can be added PRN for breakthrough pain. Instruct patients to take one or two puffs PRN up to every two hours if it does not interfere with their daily responsibilities. Most chronic pain users find sufficient pain relief this way.

If this is not enough and the patient finds themselves inhaling at regular two-hour intervals, a scheduled oral dose should be taken twice daily

---

[27] Elphick MR, Egertová M. The neurobiology and evolution of cannabinoid signalling. *Philos Trans R Soc Lond B Biol Sci.* 2001;356(1407):381–408. doi:10.1098/rstb.2000.0787.

to provide long-acting relief. The starting dose of oral THC should be 12.5mg PO BID and can be titrated upwards if necessary. In this way, THC is used similar to opioid medications like oxycodone. A short-acting dose is provided on an as-needed basis in the form of inhaled THC and a long-acting dose constitutes the baseline pain control in the form of oral THC. This combination is necessary only in patients that are in severe chronic debilitating pain.

Fibromyalgia

Marijuana is especially conducive to relieving fibromyalgia,[28] which is a disorder of hypersensitive neuronal relaying of pain signals.[29] THC causes interneuronal pathway potentiation to go extinct and resets the intensity of pain signals. To date, the best treatment for fibromyalgia is to increase physical activity, particularly activity with body contact in order to desensitize pain receptors. Disease severity increases when patients stay in bed and shield these receptors from activation, triggering pain neuron potentiation and hypersensitivity. Always instruct fibromyalgia patients to carefully combine their marijuana treatment with physical activity and tell them that it functions better this way. This is true because treatment can alleviate anxiety and helps overcome mental barriers prohibiting physical activity. A physically active patient can gain control over their fibromyalgia and also the trajectory of their overall health.

Neuropathic pain

Neuropathic pain, like diabetic neuropathy, requires higher doses of THC than other forms of pain. Since neuropathy is the result of irreversible damage to nerves rather than an inflammatory response, THC exerts most of its effects by activating CB1 receptors of interneuronal pathways, modulating neuronal potentiation. This mechanism is the same for THC's antiepileptic properties, which may not be coincidental if we consider the

---

[28] Giorgi V, Bongiovanni S, Atzeni F, Marotto D, Salaffi F, Sarzi-Puttini P. Adding medical cannabis to standard analgesic treatment for fibromyalgia: a prospective observational study. *Clin Exp Rheumatol.* 2020 Jan-Feb;38 Suppl 123(1):53-59. Epub: 2020 Feb 5. PubMed PMID: 32116208.

[29] Ngian GS, Guymer EK, Littlejohn GO. The use of opioids in fibromyalgia. *Int J Rheum Dis.* 2011;14(1):6–11. doi:10.1111/j.1756-185X.2010.01567.x.

mechanism of gabapentin and how it functions as an antiepileptic and neuropathy drug. If topical THC products are ineffective, they should be escalated to systemic forms. Both oral and inhaled therapy should be attempted but almost never achieve complete relief. Patients should be reminded of this, so they do not use too much THC in the hope of completely removing all neuropathic pain sensation.

There are some forms of neuropathy that patients have told me respond well to THC. I have encountered reports from patients of success treating tinnitus using systemic THC, either inhaled or orally. Some patients have almost complete cessation while under the effects of cannabis though I am unsure if this result is sustainable with chronic use. Also, post-herpetic neuralgia is a superficial neuropathic syndrome that has been treated well with topical and systemic THC. Studies need to be performed to determine whether long-term neuropathic pain can be decreased if post-herpetic neuralgia is treated with topical and/or systemic THC at the onset of symptoms.

Abortive Therapy

Treatment for reoccurring severe transient pain, like in trigeminal neuralgia, migraine headaches, and gout attacks should be macrodosed to help abort the symptoms as quickly as possible. Oral THC has too slow of an onset to be useful for such conditions. Inhaling vapor from THC concentrates using a vaporizer or oilrig is appropriate for administering sufficient doses. Treatment this way provides enough THC to tolerate the intense pain of these conditions and can occasionally be abortive, completely stopping their onset. For example, patients who medicate at the onset of pre-migraine auras can prevent their migraine pain from occurring.

Opiate Dependency

Marijuana relieves the symptoms of opioid withdrawal and empowers patients to tolerate abstinence. Patients require high THC doses for opiate withdrawal during weaning. This helps counter the various symptoms experienced while opioids are discontinued (hyperalgesia, anxiety, insomnia, nausea, vomiting, etc.). Once off opioids completely, marijuana can be discontinued or used in smaller amounts to treat pain and other conditions. This way, if the patient has a craving and feels like relapsing, they can reach for a vape pen instead of a needle.

Unlike with benzodiazepines and alcohol, stopping opiates completely is not deadly and I encourage it to my patients. Remind them that they can free themselves of opioid dependency by doing so themselves, without the help of their physicians from pain management or methadone clinics. The symptoms are extremely severe but stopping cold turkey and treating symptoms with cannabis yields the greatest results in my experience. Even if a patient is unable to continue, they are to take the smallest possible opioid/narcotic dose and no more. Allow patients as much cannabis as they may need while withdrawing and tell them to stock up on supplies. It will make hyperalgesia more tolerable.

Besides helping their hyperalgesia, THC has well documented antiemetic properties, for which it has been FDA approved and sold under the brand name Marinol®. One of the outstanding properties of THC is that it can be administered through inhalation during emesis and dry heaving, when oral medications would be expelled. This provides some relief so that the patient can drink and hydrate themselves.

Another method of weaning a patient off of opioids is combining THC with a buprenorphine taper. Stopping cold-turkey without medication-assisted treatment is no easy feat and buprenorphine tapering can assist patients by prolonging the withdrawal period and lowering the intensity of symptoms. I recommend a 7-10-day tapering period with buprenorphine that, when combined with THC, allows a more controlled method of discontinuing opioids. Obviously, in the best-case scenarios this is combined with counseling and rehabilitation to lower chances of relapse. One day, patients will be able to go to rehabs where THC treatment is utilized to improve success rates, exceeding results of abstinence-based models that current rehabs use.

I recommend closer follow-ups with opioid-dependent patients since they are the highest risk for overdosing, especially if they relapse. After a period of close follow-ups, the length of time between appointments can be increased unless there are red flags present. In my experience, patients in need of help from opiate dependency are happy to cooperate with any additional measures for their safety, including close monitoring.

9 OTHER CONDITIONS

Autoimmune Disease

When I started my career as a marijuana specialist, I was uncertain how often patients should administer THC for conditions like IBD. Was daily dosing warranted in all cases?

Autoimmune diseases manifest as chronic inflammation with intermittent spikes of disease activity. Irreversible microcellular insults accumulate into macroscopic lesions and permanent symptoms. This can be prevented by sustaining a basal anti-inflammatory action with THC. To slow disease progression, patients are advised to use low-dose oral THC two to three times daily even when their condition is controlled. Flare-ups can be relieved more aggressively with supplemental inhalation or additional oral doses, depending on the patient's comfort. Obviously, this should be in combination with traditional treatment.

Due to a lack of research, I am still uncertain whether the therapeutic effects of THC on autoimmune disease are dose dependent. It is worth considering titrating oral doses upwards as a prophylaxis to suppress acute flair-ups in refractory cases that are otherwise difficult to treat. Titration can stop once disease activity is controlled or side-effects overcome symptom relief.

THC Effect	Dose Provided
Basal Anti-inflammation decreases disease progression	Low-dose oral
Acute Anti-inflammation	Inhaled Q2hrs
Flare-up prophylaxis	High-dose oral THC TID

Inflammatory Bowel Disease (IBD)

In one study, ten out of eleven treatment-refractory Crohn's disease patients benefited significantly from THC.[30] Subjects were given joints with normal marijuana in the treatment group and marijuana that was THC-free in the control group. Based on what we know about the immunomodulatory effects of THC, we can assume similar outcomes for treatment of ulcerative colitis, and I have seen such results in my patients with both forms of IBD.

As mentioned, THC treatment for IBD has been studied using inhaled administration, the preferred route of most patients. It is unclear if consuming THC orally is preferable to inhaled therapy. In my opinion, oral THC may have a localized effect on the gastric tissue proximal to its absorption in the ileum alongside hydrophobic products of lipid digestion. Patients with gastrointestinal inflammation distal to THC absorption, like in ulcerative colitis, are less likely to benefit from any localized effects of THC on gastrointestinal tissue. Intestinally absorbed THC is transported in chylomicrons interstitially via lymphatic drainage to the thoracic duct, traversing enteric lymphocytes and suppressing overactivity to autoantigens via CB2-receptor-mediated mechanisms. For these reasons, oral THC is indicated for initial treatment of suspected intestinal inflammation[31] and can be titrated up or supplemented with inhalation according to clinical response to treatment and personal preferences. Flare-ups of IBD can be treated with 12.5mg or more of THC combined with one or two puffs of inhaled THC to suppress inflammation while the oral dose takes effect.

Irritable Bowel Syndrome

The gastrointestinal tract is innervated extrinsically by the sympathetic and parasympathetic nervous system (vagus and pelvic nerves) and intrinsically by myenteric and submucosal plexuses. IBS occurs from an imbalance of these complex regulatory mechanisms and, like in other organ systems, THC can be used to restore homeostasis. Direct activation of

---

[30] Naftali T, Schleider LBL, Dotan I, Lansky EP, Benjaminov FS, Konikoff FM. Cannabis induces a clinical response in patients with Crohn's disease: a prospective placebo-controlled study. *Clin Gastroenterol Hepatol.* 2013:11(10):1276-1280. doi:10.1016/j.cgh.2013.04.034.

[31] Including celiac and eosinophilic esophagitis/gastritis, etc.

presynaptic CB1-receptors inhibits long-term potentiation[32] and this may be responsible for resynchronizing the rhythm of circular and longitudinal smooth muscle contractions.[33]

THC also has indirect psychological benefits because IBS is greatly influenced by emotional factors via the extrinsic autonomic nervous system on large intestinal motility. Psychiatric illness or anxiety precedes IBS symptoms in two thirds of people with IBS. Emotional triggers of IBS can be controlled by inhaling THC during times of stress.

Additionally, THC may have long-term beneficial effects on appetite that are conducive for IBS symptom relief, such as meal regularity. Instructing patients to use cannabis before meals and instructing them not to snack between meals can create a healthier lifestyle and improved regulation of dietary intake.

Patients have reported improvement of IBS symptoms when treatment is administered orally in conjunction with their meals. Recommend starting low dose THC orally with their largest meals to synchronize therapy with gastric motility. After 6-8 weeks of successful therapy, suggest de-escalating scheduled oral therapy to an as-needed basis. This has produced the best results for IBS control in my patients.

Cancer

Cancer patients can use marijuana for improving the odds of remission, psychological relief and, at the very least, to alleviate symptoms of chemotherapy and radiation. The immunomodulating effects of cannabis may have antineoplastic properties that improve success rates of chemotherapy. Since no one has ever died from too much THC consumption, any antineoplastic effects present in THC can be maximized

---

[32] Silva-Cruz A, Carlström M, Ribeiro JA, Sebastião AM. Dual Influence of Endocannabinoids on Long-Term Potentiation of Synaptic Transmission. *Front Pharmacol.* 2017;8:921. doi:10.3389/fphar.2017.00921. eCollection 2017. PubMed PMID: 29311928; PubMed Central PMCID: PMC5742107.

[33] Rohof WO, Aronica E, Beaumont H, Troost D, Boeckxstaens GE. Localization of mGluR5, GABAB, GABAA, and cannabinoid receptors on the vago-vagal reflex pathway responsible for transient lower esophageal sphincter relaxation in humans: an immunohistochemical study". *Neurogastroenterol Motil.* 2012 Apr;*24*(4):383-e173. doi:10.1111/j.1365-2982.2011.01868.x. Epub: 2012 Jan 19. PubMed PMID: 22256945.

by high doses. If remission is the goal, doses of THC should be titrated as quickly as possible and limited only by patient intolerance to medication side-effects. Oral cannabis products are most suitable for administering THC at sufficient doses. This protocol was first popularized in Canada by Rick Simpson. His results treating cancer patients with rapidly increasing doses titrated to patient tolerance persuaded him to openly confess his observations to authorities years before Canadian cannabis prohibition was abolished.

Cannabis treatment should be used in conjunction with conventional protocols because both modes of therapy mutually benefit one another. THC at the very least improves chemotherapy completion rates by improving side-effect tolerance. In addition, the antineoplastic properties of THC are more likely to be effective when the cancer is weakened by pharmaceuticals and radiation. Probably for these reasons my most profound success stories have been in those treated with conventional treatments and high-dose THC simultaneously. I have seen cases of glioblastoma multiforme and stage IV hepatocellular carcinoma go into remission after treatment with conventional medicine in combination with high-dose THC.

Patients with lung cancer are encouraged to vaporize THC in conjunction with oral treatment to take advantage of any local effects of THC on the tumor cells. This may be controversial but the lack of detrimental effects of vaporizing THC on lung function suggests that it is safe to allow this.

Remind patients that they do not need their oncologist's permission to use cannabis treatment. Studies about cannabis use have been blocked by the government so the lack of research often delays approval by oncologists to permit their patients to use cannabis products. Because cannabis is relatively harmless and allows patients to tolerate chemotherapy better, patients should not delay THC treatment by waiting for their oncologist to agree to its use.

Radiological Monitoring

Prior to initiating therapy, it's important to carefully examine MRI and CT studies to determine the rate at which the cancer is progressing. This will enable a clearer determination of treatment efficacy down the line. Consider prior and ongoing therapy and any changes that are planned in conjunction with initiating THC. All these effects on cancer progression need to be considered to assess treatment benefit since no guidelines exist and each case is different.

Usually, patients will have sequential imaging studies ordered by oncologists and patients can be advised to have the results faxed or brought to follow up appointments. The rate of tumor growth is one of the most important objective measurements of THC efficacy. If tumor growth has stopped or the size regressed, treatment can be continued. If tumor growth has continued but slowed, treatment can continue or be de-escalated depending on the patient's preferences and goals of care.

Tumor factors should also be carefully monitored and noted at appointments. Multiple prostate cancer patients have come to me for marijuana cards after observing a drop in AFP following marijuana treatment.

In end-stage cancer, patients may choose to accept defeat and die a comfortable death. This is the time to de-escalate cannabis treatment to symptomatic relief. This usually means titrating treatment to a dose with the least undesirable effects. If a tolerance has been developed, patients may remain at moderate-to-high doses and adjusted based on symptom control. An acceptable THC dose for such a patient would be 50mg by mouth two to three times daily with one-to-two puffs inhaled as-needed for break-through nausea, pain or anxiety. Marijuana is one of the most important medications for end-of-life care because it provides both somatic and psychological relief. Allow patients to use as much as they deem necessary at this time.

Depression

Depression may be a result of dysfunction of the endocannabinoid system.[34] Traditionally, cannabis was associated with depression and thought to worsen it. Over time, however, it is becoming clearer that cannabis users are not depressed because they use cannabis, but instead they use cannabis to treat their depression.

As is evident from the initial giggles witnessed in new users,

---

[34] Ashton CH, Moore PB. Endocannabinoid system dysfunction in mood and related disorders. *Acta Psychiatr Scand.* 2011 Oct;*124*(4):250-61. doi:10.1111/j.1600-0447.2011.01687.x. Epub: 2011 Mar 9. Review. PubMed PMID: 21916860.

marijuana affects the areas in our brain that control our mood and overall mental well-being. Whether we want to admit it or not, most people today are at least mildly depressed and occasionally anxious. THC helps alleviate these problems by stabilizing our thoughts and cognitive state-of-being. Marijuana has been shown to improve depressionin a prospective observational study.[35] As would be expected, THC alone was more effective than treatment with a lower dose of THC combined with CBD. Both treatments contained the active ingredient but in different amounts, suggesting a dose-dependent effect on improving depression.

I recommend to patients who are depressed to use marijuana in two ways. One is to alleviate their daily psychological stress by using an inhaled dose of marijuana before bed. This helps them cope with the day's events and prepare fresh for the next day's responsibilities. It also grounds them and provides them an opportunity for introspection and self-reflection, finding a meaning to their lives, or more easily accepting a lack of one. At first, they may have some groundbreaking realizations and in time they will secure their identity and value their self-worth. At the very least, it allows them time to relax without over-thinking and stressing about their lives.

The second way to use marijuana for depression is to administer at times of acute emotional turmoil. This helps stabilize emotions, especially when combined with a short break to recoup. Patients can be instructed to inhale THC when they are emotional and, if possible, revisit the circumstance leading to their emotional state after the THC wares off. This will calm them through hormonal homeostasis restoration and allow time to reconsider their initial viewpoints and reaction.

Marijuana is also a safe treatment for acute grief. I recommend low-dose oral treatment scheduled with as-needed inhalation. Oral THC doses can start at 12.5mg and be increased to 25mg but should not require more than this for most patients. The purpose of treatment is to stabilize patients, not to wash away their sorrows.

---

[35] Giorgi V, Bongiovanni S, Atzeni F, Marotto D, Salaffi F, Sarzi-Puttini P. Adding medical cannabis to standard analgesic treatment for fibromyalgia: a prospective observational study. *Clin Exp Rheumatol.* 2020 Jan-Feb;38 Suppl 123(1):53-59. Epub: 2020 Feb 5. PubMed PMID: 32116208.

Finally, marijuana may be helpful even in the most severe desperation. It would not surprise me if suicidal patients may find benefit from using marijuana in the acute phase of a suicidal breakdown. More research is needed to determine if THC can abort suicidal ideation and stave off inpatient psychiatric hospitalization. Unlike alcohol, THC is an inhibiting drug that may prevent patients from acting on their suicidal thoughts.

PTSD

Patients with PTSD are recommended to treat readily in high amounts. Patients find the most benefit if they prepare for unexpected and unpredictable triggers prophylactically. When patients medicate with marijuana, they raise their threshold for when a trigger elicits an autonomic response. Whenever possible, patients should try a moderate oral dose two to three times a day for trigger prophylaxis. Doses of THC can start at 25mg and increased to 50mg or more, depending on practitioner discretion.

Predictable events that may cause post-traumatic episodes should be managed by administering doses prior to the trigger. Patients can choose whether to use oral or inhaled administration and guidance should be provided based on the patient's lifestyle, severity of illness and the timing of the events (i.e., family reunion vs crossing bridges, etc.).

Instruct patients to terminate post-traumatic episodes they are unable to prevent with the use of high-dose inhaled THC. Optimally, patients should use a wax-pen filled with marijuana concentrates, which delivers higher doses more rapidly than pens using pre-filled cannabis oil cartridges. Alternatively, dabbing concentrates with an oil rig can abort a post-traumatic episode. Patients can administer as many doses as they feel necessary to maintain composure and regain peace of mind.

Sexual Dysfunction

According to accounts of patients, multiple disorders of sexual dysfunction are treatable with cannabis to vastly improve quality of life. THC restores homeostasis to sexual desire and may serve as an aphrodisiac for those with hypoactive sexual desire disorder (HSSD).[36] THC relieves

---

[36] Mondino A, Fernández S, Garcia-Carnelli C. *et al.* Vaporized Cannabis differentially modulates sexual behavior of female rats according to the dose. *Pharmacol Biochem Behav.*

situational psychological stressors, like those driving erectile dysfunction and vaginismus. Additionally, there may be beneficial effects on the vascular circulation and neuronal tactile sensitivity that occurs in the genitals following arousal and during intercourse. Inhaling THC at moderate-to-high doses before sex has optimal duration since it will provide a window of two hours for intercourse.

THC has no appreciable systemic absorption across mucous membranes but THC-containing lubricants can provide local anti-inflammatory effects and may relieve pelvic tension in women. Oil-based products can be applied before intercourse to enhance foreplay and allow the THC time to become locally active. Very few THC-infused lubricants have been developed and tested, so warn patients to take caution by trying a small amount first. Such products can potentially improve quality of life dramatically in the bedroom.

HIV

While there remains little research into the long-term effects of THC on the health of HIV patients, its CB2 receptor activity may provide beneficial effects that counter the slow deterioration caused by chronic inflammation from a persistent infection by the virus.

HIV creates an inflammatory state that predisposes patients to chronic conditions like atherosclerosis and cancer. This presents an overall picture of accelerated aging. Like in autoimmune diseases, persistent antigen-specific exposure disrupts the immune system's balance between activation and prevention of excessive immune-mediated damage. Secretion of proinflammatory cytokines creates microcellular injury, particularly to the endothelial cells, causing premature cardiovascular disease and higher rates of certain cancers, diabetes, renal and hepatic disease,[37][38] and neurocognitive

---

2019 Dec;187:172814. doi:10.1016/j.pbb.2019.172814. Epub: 2019 Oct 20. PubMed PMID: 31644886.

[37] Wyatt CM. Kidney Disease and HIV Infection. *Top Antivir Med.* 2017;25(1):13-16. PMID: 28402929; PMCID: PMC5677039.

[38] Sherman KE, Rockstroh J, Thomas D. Human immunodeficiency virus and liver disease: An update. *Hepatology.* 2015;62(6):1871-1882. doi:10.1002/hep.28150.

dysfunction,[39] among other conditions. Daily THC administration may alleviate this chronic inflammation of HIV infection by modulating immune system activity to prevent irreversible microcellular damage through CB2 receptor activation.

Low dose oral THC administration in the morning and evening will provide coverage in the day and night to help slow progression of HIV-associated illnesses. In the weeks following the start of treatment, a rise in CD8+ T-cell count and a drop in HIV viral load is expected and reflects medication efficacy.

Epilepsy

The medical community has been led to believe that the antiepileptic effects of cannabis comes from CBD. Initially, the driver for this was to find a non-psychoactive constituent to marijuana. A Colorado CBD company declared that they cured a child of refractory seizures using a low-THC, high-CBD strain that they named "Charlotte's Web," after the young girl.[40] Families began moving to Colorado to treat their own children. Meanwhile, a pharmaceutical company called GW Pharmaceuticals began conducting their own studies, led by Orrin Devinsky, MD, who was also Charlotte's doctor. These large, international studies on pediatric refractory epilepsy confirmed the reports from families by establishing a significant decrease in seizure frequency.[41] Since CBD was approved by the FDA, secondary opinion pieces lacking primary research are being published in support of CBD.

My experiences treating epileptic patients has led me to believe that we are barking up the wrong tree in regard to CBD. Many patients at Nature's Way Medicine have successfully substituted multiple antiepileptic drugs with high-THC marijuana. None have been able to do this using CBD.

---

[39] Clifford DB, Ances BM. HIV-associated neurocognitive disorder. *Lancet Infect Dis.* 2013;13(11):976-986. doi:10.1016/S1473-3099(13)70269-X.

[40] Stanley J. The surprising story of medical marijuana and pediatric epilepsy. YouTube. https://www.youtube.com/watch?v=ciQ4ErmhO7g. Accessed: May 3, 2019.

[41] Devinsky O, Cross JH, Laux L. *et al.* Trial of Cannabidiol for Drug-Resistant Seizures in the Dravet Syndrome. *N Engl J Med.* 2017 May 25;376(21):2011-2020. doi:10.1056/NEJMoa1611618. PubMed PMID: 28538134.

A report by CNN medical correspondent Sanjay Gupta revealed that Charlotte's epilepsy continues to threaten her life more than ever.[42] Following the Devinsky study, a letter to the New England Journal of Medicine by Chinese physicians was skeptical of GW pharmaceuticals' CBD research by questioning the validity of the authors' conclusions, pointing out that CBD inhibits CYP450 3A drug clearance.[43] Their concern was that the reported drop in seizure frequency was indirectly caused by a rise in serum concentration of concomitantly administered antiepileptics and their active metabolites, rather than a direct action of CBD itself.

After carefully following my established well-controlled epileptics managed with THC, I have formed the opinion that families traveling to Colorado to treat their children's epilepsy must also be administering THC to them. Given the marijuana industry's poor quality control, products contaminated with THC are probably being used and considered to be entirely CBD. Alternatively, some families are administering THC to their children under the guise of CBD, fearing ramifications by social services.

If THC controls epilepsy by activating the CB1 receptor, a CB1 antagonist would be detrimental to a seizure patient. CBD is an antagonist, not an agonist of the CB1 receptor. Contrary to current popular opinion, treating epilepsy with CBD is more likely to harm patients. I believe that I have had patients on at least two occasions have life-threatening status epilepticus after switching from THC to CBD for seizure management. This is because the patients switched from a CBD agonist (THC) to an antagonist (CBD). For this reason, I always explain to seizure patients that they should adhere to THC despite popular belief that CBD is effective. I recommend notifying local dispensary pharmacists that your seizure patients are to only receive THC products. Whenever possible, utilize your state's marijuana program protocols to protect patients from being advised to use CBD by budtenders. For example, you may be able to provide special instructions on their marijuana certifications that specify to only sell them THC products,

---

[42] Gupta S. CNN Weed 3: The Marijuana Revolution. YouTube. https://www.youtube.com/watch?v=jpd5Gz_5_G8. Accessed: May 1, 2020.

[43] Tang R, Fang F. Trial of Cannabidiol for Drug-Resistant Seizures in the Dravet Syndrome. *N Engl J Med*. 2017 Aug 17;377(7):699. doi:10.1056/NEJMc1708349. PubMed PMID: 28816426.

never CBD.

Epilepsy protocol

Advise patients to continue their current antiepileptic drugs (AEDs) until after THC therapy is initiated. Any CBD use should be discontinued. Most patients prefer inhalation over oral administration and self-medicate throughout the day as much as their lifestyle permits. Some patients prefer to use oral THC in conjunction with inhaling. Always advise them to share their goals of treatment with their neurologists who will monitor their progress.

The dose of THC should be titrated upwards to a level of psychoactivity that does not adversely affect their quality of life. Once on a stable regimen of THC, other antiepileptics can be weaned off, one at a time. Interdisciplinary teamwork is advised between the patient's other healthcare practitioners monitoring their treatment because patients will be at highest risk for seizures when coming off of their old antiepileptic drugs. In fact, it can be expected that patients will eventually have a breakthrough seizure because if and when they discontinue their traditional AEDs, the THC should also be titrated down to the lowest amounts necessary for complete seizure control. Once a seizure occurs, the THC dose can be readjusted to a level higher than the one that caused a breakthrough seizure. Patients should be advised not to drive during this high-risk period of medication adjustment to ensure they don't have a motor vehicle accident.

Driving

Because epileptic patients transitioning to THC are almost certain to have a seizure while transitioning to long-term THC maintenance, I advise my patients not to drive until an optimal regimen is found. If their seizures are controlled with THC use, driving can be restarted. Patients with epilepsy who are on stable THC treatment should be not be discouraged from driving after using THC because its effects on performance are negligible compared to the risk of inciting a seizure from a lapse in antiepileptic coverage.

Since state laws prohibit patients from driving while under the influence of THC, these recommendations are based on Hippocratic criteria. In my experience, judges side with patients who are supported by a doctor's letter explaining the circumstances and need for treatment. Have courage if called on for help and write letters supporting patients that are behaving and medicating appropriately. Patients employed as commercial drivers will depend on you for such letters to keep their jobs. Do not start a commercial driver on marijuana if you do not plan on writing letters of support because employers in this industry are still uncertain whether to comply with state marijuana laws and will fire marijuana card-holders if they are unable to provide a letter of support from their recommending physician. If the patient is not an epileptic, instruct them to only use marijuana after driving and clarify that in any letters to their employers.

Autism

Patients with autism present somewhere along the spectrum from mild Asperger's syndrome to overt cognitive dysfunction from developmental delays. Less severe forms present as individuals with poor social skills. Such mild cases can use marijuana to decrease anxiety and prevent introverted over-thinking while socializing. Encourage patients to use THC for improving their natural reactions and responses during social interactions. Warn them that they may have increased paranoia while they become familiar with using marijuana. Occasionally, marijuana can make autistic social awkwardness worse, especially when beginning treatment. This usually changes after becoming familiar with the effects and once a tolerance is developed.

Autism with *Self-injury*

Severe cases of autism require caretakers to urgently manage emotional outbursts that may involve aggression and self-injurious behaviors. Preventing episodes like this can be attempted with prophylactic low-dose oral treatment twice daily and titrated upwards based on response. Urgent management to abort an emotional episode involving self-injury by the patient can be attempted using inhalation treatment. Instruct caregivers to prepare patients by educating them to self-administer vaporized THC at a time when they are calm and receptive to learning. When a tantrum occurs, patients will know how to self-administer and will need less assistance.

Vape pens containing pre-filled oil cartridges with airflow-triggered vaporization are easier to operate than vaporizers with buttons and adjustable controls. In resilient cases, wax-pens that vaporize concentrates are preferred because they produce higher-potency THC vapor. Caretakers can pre-load chambers with vapor before handing it to patients for use. Severely mentally disabled patients will require a facemask to passively inhale vapor during respiration, though such devices for inhaling THC haven't been developed yet.

Dementia

My earliest use of THC on patients was on demented, critically ill patients in the ICU who I treated with dronabinol. These patients were most often prescribed this as a last resort to restore their will to live. These patients convinced me of THC's value by regaining an appetite and recovering enough energy to leave the ICU. Despite their age, dementia, critical illness, and many medications, the patients were always able to tolerate the treatment without becoming delirious.

Dementia should be treated with routine low-dose oral THC to slow disease progression by lowering immune-mediated apoptosis, thus preserving neurons. It will also be useful for depression and insomnia, some of the earliest presenting symptoms of dementia. Unfortunately, my patients have not found significant benefit using marijuana for movement control, aside from secondary effects of decreased psychological stress, anxiety and over-thinking voluntary actions. These symptoms are a result of irreversible neuronal death. Similar lackluster results treating muscle spasms suggests that the corticospinal tracts are relatively unaffected by THC compared to somatosensory pathways.

End-of-Life Care

The final stages of dementia and hospice care warrants de-escalating treatment to purely symptomatic relief. Patients eventually become completely disoriented and dysfunctional. Comfort and agitation can be better controlled with routine administration of low-to-moderate dose THC. If oral intake is no longer possible, administration through percutaneous endoscopic gastrostomy (PEG) tubes will suffice. For this I recommend cannabis oils sold in syringes. Make sure the oil has been processed to decarboxylate its THCA into physiologically active THC. Cannabis oils are very sticky and flushing with a small amount of linseed oil before and after the dose of THC helps prevent clogging the feeding tube.

Sepsis

Many of the patients I treated in the ICU for dementia were suffering from severe sepsis with end organ dysfunction. At the time, I felt the dronabinol I was using on them improved their conditions because of its psychological effects. However, I cannot exclude the effect that THC has on the immune system in their recoveries. By binding the CB2 receptor, THC may have been lowering inflammation and immune reactivity, allowing the body to clear the infection more easily. At this point, these are merely speculations but in time we might discover that the immunomodulatory effects of THC may prove useful in controlling the inflammatory cascade and cytokine storm in sepsis patients. In the past, we have attempted using corticosteroids for similar reasons. Cannabis may prove more beneficial once studies are allowed to take place.

Pediatric Patients

Parents bringing their children for marijuana treatment must be catered to extra carefully. These families are usually against THC, seeking a non-psychoactive alternative. They must be educated on the absence of other clinically relevant cannabinoids and comforted with reassurance that THC will not harm the child or hinder their development. The purpose of THC is to enhance the child's chances of success. Each case requires careful consideration of treatment by weighing the potential benefits to adverse effects on the child's psychological well-being, academic performance, and social skills. You will have to explain that effective treatment with THC will cause the child to feel high, but this is not a cause for concern because it denotes therapeutic activity.

Instruct children to keep their treatment private. Schools are still very sensitive about marijuana therapy so keeping treatment private prevents undue stress and helps protect the child's emotional well-being.

Pregnancy

Some patients can be helped with medical marijuana during pregnancy. It is always better to err on the side of caution to protect the fetus, but, in some instances, I have found marijuana to be useful. For example, women with PTSD who stop THC when they become pregnant are at risk of miscarriage. Continuing treatment can prevent this. If a woman has had multiple miscarriages after discontinuing marijuana because she became pregnant, it may be worthwhile attempting to continue marijuana to preserve the pregnancy.

I have not witnessed any detrimental effects in babies exposed to THC in utero, unlike other drugs, which cause well-known sequelae in newborns. For this reason, I have little hesitation advising patients to use THC while pregnant when the treatment can alleviate symptoms of severe morning sickness or other conditions. The beneficial effects to the mother and the fetus outweigh theoretical possibilities of harm in such circumstances. There have been studies that suggest a lower birth weight in babies born to mothers who use cannabis; however, these effects do not last because there is catch-up growth, at least in rat models.[44]

Hemodialysis

Only about 20% of THC is excreted in the urine and renal failure does not change the duration of action of THC. It may slightly increase the window in which THC is detectable in body fluids but the high will still last about 2 hours after inhalation and 5 hours after ingestion.

Patients with end-stage renal disease experience malaise both before and after hemodialysis. Before dialysis, there is a build-up of inflammatory byproducts and other molecules that would ordinarily be excreted by the kidneys. Afterwards, their bodies are drained of energy. Recommending to patients that they take marijuana orally the morning of dialysis is especially useful for patients. The longer duration of action will last throughout the procedure at a time when inflammation is especially high in their bodies. Patients become less restless while they wait 3-4 hours to complete their dialysis.

---

[44] Natale BV, Gustin KN, Lee K, *et al.* Δ9-tetrahydrocannabinol exposure during rat pregnancy leads to symmetrical fetal growth restriction and labyrinth-specific vascular defects in the placenta. *Sci Rep.* 2020;10(1):544. Published 2020 Jan 17. doi:10.1038/s41598-019-57318-6.

COPD

Studies examining whether marijuana causes COPD have been mixed.[45] Marijuana on its own has not been definitively shown to cause COPD but when used in conjunction with tobacco the effects are more than tobacco alone.[46] This means that it is especially important for patients to quit smoking cigarettes if they use medical marijuana. It is recommended to counsel patients to substitute tobacco with marijuana products and stress the need to discontinue smoking cigarettes to preserve their lung function.

Many physicians are afraid to recommend inhaling marijuana to patients with COPD. It has been my experience that this is not something to be afraid of. Out of caution, it is best that these patients vaporize marijuana products rather than smoke it. This prevents the inhalation of unwanted products of combustion.

While there is no scientific evidence at this time to suggest a positive effect on lung function in patients who vaporize with marijuana, I can say that I have witnessed patients improve in their oxygen requirements after starting to vaporize marijuana. Patients on 4 liters of continuous O_2 through their nasal canula have gone down to 2 liters, or using it only at night. This has occurred in about a dozen patients of mine and almost every patient that was on oxygen at the time of starting. These patients were no longer tobacco users and, according to the scientific literature, I expect that their oxygen requirements would have worsened rather than improved had they been concomitant tobacco smokers.

It is premature to suggest that vaporizing marijuana products may be useful in patients with compromised lung function. The mechanism by which that could happen is uncertain and would be only speculative. However, from my experience with patients vaporizing marijuana while on oxygen, it is my opinion that physicians should not be afraid to allow COPD patients to inhale THC.

One important caution, however, is to ensure that the products the

---

[45] Tashkin DP. Does smoking marijuana increase the risk of chronic obstructive pulmonary disease?. *CMAJ*. 2009;180(8):797–798. doi:10.1503/cmaj.090142.

[46] Tan WC, Lo C, Jong A, *et al*. Marijuana and chronic obstructive lung disease: a population-based study. *CMAJ*. 2009;180(8):814–820. doi:10.1503/cmaj.081040.

patients are using pose no danger to combusting when in proximity of supplemental oxygen flow. The risk is small but certain vaporizers may be at risk of exposing their coils to oxygen and potentially causing a risk of fire. Typical vape-pens composed of batteries for replaceable cartridges are unlikely to pose this risk.

Glaucoma

Intraocular pressure has been significantly lowered in studies using THC as a treatment modality. In one study, an experimental mouse model of glaucoma was treated with systemic THC through injection and the results showed a significant preservation of retinal ganglion cells through lowering of the intraocular pressure.[47] In another study, dogs were treated with topical ophthalmic solution containing 2% THC, resulting in a moderate decrease in intraocular pressure. Studies like these have resulted in many states allowing patients to use medical marijuana for glaucoma.

Closed-angle glaucoma in the acute stages is a medical emergency and should not be treated with cannabis. However, open-angle glaucoma can be treated with THC treatment. Patients have reported to me that their intraocular pressure readings have gone down after starting daily cannabis treatment for their glaucoma. All of these patients were using cannabis systemically, through inhalation or oral consumption. It would be useful for the cannabis industry to create ophthalmic solution containing THC, like in the study mentioned above. This would be a wonderful opportunity to use THC to treat glaucoma without the experience of being high from systemic administration. Hopefully, in the future physicians will be able to recommend ophthalmic THC eye drops to patients with glaucoma.

---

[47] Crandall J, Matragoon S, Khalifa YM, Borlongan C, Tsai NT, Caldwell RB, Liou GI. Neuroprotective and intraocular pressure-lowering effects of (-)Delta9-tetrahydrocannabinol in a rat model of glaucoma. *Ophthalmic Res.* 2007;39(2):69-75. doi:10.1159/000099240. Epub: 2007 Feb 2. PubMed PMID: 17284931.

ABOUT THE AUTHOR

Matthew Roman, MD is an internal medicine board certified physician. He has a bachelor's degree from Franklin & Marshall College in neuroscience with a minor in chemistry. He studied medicine at Jagiellonian University in Cracow, Poland in a socialized healthcare system. After completing his residency at UPMC Mercy Hospital in Pittsburgh, Pennsylvania he worked as a hospitalist. He has specialized in medical marijuana since opening a clinic in Wilmington, Delaware in 2015 that integrated primary care with cannabis. Since then, he has moved his practice to Old City Philadelphia, where he has trained other physicians as medical marijuana specialists. In the future, Dr. Roman hopes to open a detox center for opioid addiction that uses THC to treat withdrawal symptoms and prevent relapse.

GLOSSARY

Atomizer – The part on a vaporizer that contains heat coils to vaporize concentrates.

Banger – A quartz glass nail shaped like a mug that is used with an oil rig to vaporize concentrates. It is heated with a torch first and covered with a carb cap to increase vaporization efficiency.

Blunt – A hand-rolled cigar with marijuana flower inside of it. Usually rolled with the outside leaf of a tobacco cigar.

Bong – A water pipe that stands upright and has a downstem that reaches below the water level so smoke is cooled and filtered through the water. It is first filled with smoke that is inhaled afterwards to clear the pipe with fresh air.

Bowl – The part of a pipe that is packed with marijuana flower.

Budtender – A dispensary employee who sells patients marijuana and provides recommendations.

Butane Hash Oil (BHO) – Marijuana concentrate that is produced from flower by extraction using butane as the solvent.

Carb Cap – A cap, usually glass, that is placed on top of a glass nail to improve vaporization of concentrates. It allows a stream of air to be aimed at the concentrate.

CBD – Cannabidiol. A cannabinoid that does not bind CB1 or CB2 receptors and functions mostly as a placebo.

CBV – Cannabivarin. Like CBD, it is a cannabinoid that is non-psychoactive and has little clinical value.

Cherry – The ember of marijuana that is lit in the bowl of a pipe.

CO_2 Oil – Marijuana concentrate created through extraction using liquid CO_2 as the solvent.

Crystals – High-concentration THC concentrate that appears like small crystals because of the crystallization of THC.

Curing – The process of drying fresh marijuana flower to improve its quality and aroma.

Dabbing – The process of vaporizing small pieces of marijuana concentrate by inhaling them after placing them on a hot nail.

Diamonds – Pure THC crystals. The highest quality form of marijuana containing no byproducts or unnecessary ingredients.

Dime-Bag – A $10 dollar bag of marijuana.

Distillate – Distilled marijuana products that often contain additives like terpenes and CBD.

Downstem – The portion of a water pipe that extends from the bowl to the bottom of the pipe, often reaching into water to allow for filtration.

Drag – A puff or inhalation.

Edibles – Food infused with THC.

Eighth – An eighth of an ounce of marijuana. Along with individual grams, it is the most common increment that marijuana is sold in. There are 3.5 grams per eighth (of an ounce).

e-Nail – An electronically heated nail to vaporize marijuana products. It can be made from metal or quartz glass wrapped with a large electric coil to heat the glass.

EVALI – E-Cigarette or Vaping Associated Lung Injury. Also known as Vaping-Associated Pulmonary Injury (VAPI). An acute pulmonary condition that can be deadly linked to inhaling black-market marijuana products contaminated with vitamin E acetate.

Flower – The part of the cannabis plant that is smoked and contains THC.

Grinder – A device used to grind marijuana flower so it is easier to roll and smoke.

Hash – An old-fashioned form of concentrate that is black and malleable, containing too many contaminants to vaporize. Usually, it is added to marijuana flower or tobacco and smoked.

Hemp – Cannabis that is produced for nutritional or industrial purposes. Legally, it contains less than 0.3% THC.

High – The psychoactive effect of marijuana.

Indica – A strain of marijuana that has traditionally been said to have a more sedative effect, though this is unproven.

Joint – A marijuana cigarette.

Kief – The powder formed by the accumulation of dislodged trichomes from marijuana flower.

Medical – A term used for marijuana that is recommended by a physician for medical purposes.

Munchies – The acute hunger caused as a side-effect of using marijuana.

Nail – A protruding metal or quartz glass piece that is heated for concentrates to be placed onto, so they vaporize.

Nickle-Bag (or Nick-Bag) – A $5-dollar bag of marijuana.

Oil Rig – A device that a nail can be attached to. Used to vaporize concentrates. Contains water to cool the vapor. Similar to a waterpipe. Typically made of glass.

Recreational – A term used for marijuana that does not require a doctor's recommendation.

Rick Simpson Oil (RSO) – A strong marijuana concentrate made with distillation using alcohol. Classically recommended as a treatment for cancer. Usually ingested orally.

Rosin – A marijuana concentrate created from heating flower and pressing it with high pressure to squeeze out the concentrate.

Sauce – A term used for terpenes that are added to concentrates.

Sativa – A strain of marijuana that is traditionally claimed to have excitatory effects relative to its counterpart indica. This has not been proven.

Sensimilla – A term originating from Spanish that literally means, "seedless." Used for high-quality marijuana that has no seeds in it because the male cannabis plants were removed to prevent pollination of the female plants that produce marijuana flower.

Shatter – A concentrate that has a brittle consistency that causes it to shatter under pressure.

Shotgun – A small hole on a pipe that allows users to clear out the pipe's smoke with fresh air.

Sugar – Marijuana concentrate that has a high enough percentage of THC to allow for crystallization and make it appear as if it contained sugar.

Terpenes – Various organic compounds present in cannabis flower that are often marketed to have medicinal properties. In actuality, they only provide flavor and aromas.

THC – Tetrahydrocannabinol. The active ingredient in marijuana.

THCa – Tetrahydrocannabinolic acid. The inactive precursor to THC that is decarboxylated when heated to become active THC. Present in marijuana flower.

Trichomes – Small glandular outgrowths on marijuana flower that contain high amounts of THC. Almost invisible to the naked eye but can produce a sugar-coated appearance on close inspection.

Trimmers – A professional marijuana preparer that cuts leaves and stems off of marijuana flower before it is cured.

Vape Pen – An electronic device that vaporizes marijuana oil in cartridges or concentrates in a chamber containing an atomizer with heating coils.

Vaporization – The process of rapidly evaporating THC so that it can be administered through inhalation.

Wax – A marijuana concentrate that is yellow and soft, like a beeswax.

WORKS CITED

Abraham, A.D., et al. "Orally Consumed Cannabinoids Provide Long-Lasting Relief of Allodynia in a Mouse Model of Chronic Neuropathic Pain." *Neuropsychopharmacology* (2019). Print.

Alshaarawy, O., and Anthony, J.C. "Are Cannabis Users Less Likely to Gain Weight? Resullts from a National 3-Year Prospective Study." *International Journal of Epidemiology* 48.5 (2019): 1695-000. Print.

Ashton, C. H., and P. B. Moore. "Endocannabinoid System Dysfunction in Mood and Related Disorders." 124.4 (2011): 250-61. Print.

Beydogan, A.B., et al. "The Protective Effects of Δ9-Tetrahydrocannabinol against Inflammation and Oxidative Stress in Rat Liver with Fructose-Induced Hyperinsulinemia." 71.3 (2019): 408-16. Print.

Blount, B.C., et al. "Vitamin E Acetate in Bronchoalveolar-Lavage Fluid Associated with Evali." *The New England Journal of Medicine* 382.8 (2020): 697-705. Print.

Centers for Disease Control and Prevention. "Outbreak of Lung Injury Associated with E-Cigarette Use, or Vaping." 15 February 2020. Web.

Clifford, D.B., and Ances, B.M. "Hiv-Associated Neurocognitive Disorder." *The Lancet. Infectious diseases* 13.11 (2013): 976-86. Print.

Crandall J, Matragoon S, Khalifa YM, Borlongan C, Tsai NT, Caldwell RB, Liou GI. "Neuroprotective and intraocular pressure-lowering effects of (-)Delta9-tetrahydrocannabinol in a rat model of glaucoma." *Ophthalmic Research.* 2007;39(2):69-75. doi: 10.1159/000099240. Epub 2007 Feb 2. PubMed PMID: 17284931.

Devinsky, O., et al. "Trial of Cannabidiol for Drug-Resistant Seizures in the Dravet Syndrome." *New England Journal of Medicine* 376 (2017): 2011-20. Print.

Druglibrary.org. 2020. Statement Of Dr. William C. Woodward, Legislative Council, American Medical Association. [online] Available at: http://www.druglibrary.org/Schaffer/hemp/taxact/woodward.ht m [Accessed 1 May 2020].

Elphick, M.R., and Egertova, M. "The Neurobiology and Evolution of Cannabinoid Signalling." *Philosophical Transactions of the Royal Society B: Biological Sciences* 356 (2001): 381-408. Print.

Fantus, R.J., et al. "The Effect of Tetrahydrocannabinol on Testosterone among Men in the United States: Results from the National Health and Nutrition Examination Survey." *World Journal of Urology* (2020). Print.

Fischer KM, Ward DA, Hendrix DV. "Effects of a topically applied 2% delta-9-tetrahydrocannabinol ophthalmic solution on intraocular pressure and aqueous humor flow rate in clinically normal dogs." *American Journal of Veterinary Research.* 2013 Feb;74(2):275-80. doi: 10.2460/ajvr.74.2.275. PubMed PMID: 23363354.

Giorgi, V., et al. "Adding Medical Cannabis to Standard Analgesic Treatment for Fibromyalgia: A Prospective Observational Study." *Clinical and Experimental Rheumatology* 123.1 (2020 Jan-Feb): 53-59. Print.

Gupta, S. "Cnn Weed 3 "the Marijuana Revolution" Dr Sanjay Gupta Md Part 3 of 3." Canna Medical Corp, 2016. Web video.

Hartnett, K.P., et al. "Syndromic Surveillance for E-Cigarette, or Vaping, Product Use-Associated Injury." *New England Journal of Medicine* 382: 766-772. Print.

Huestis, MA. "Pharmacokinetics and Metabolism of the Plant Cannabinoids, Delta9-Tetrahydrocannabinol, Cannabidiol and Cannabinol." *Handbook of Experimental Pharmacology* 168 (2005): 657-90. Print.

Jakoi, A.M., et al. "The Effects of Marijuana Use on Lumbar Spinal Fusion." Publish Ahead of Print (2019). Print.

Le Strat, Y., and Le Foll, B. "Obesity and Cannabis Use: Results from 2 Representative National Surveys." *American Journal of Epidemiology* 174.8 (2011): 929-33. Print.

Li, H-L. "An Archaeological and Historical Account of Cannabis in China." *Economic Botany* 28.4 (1974): 437-48. Print.

Maher, R.L., et al. "Clinical Consequences of Polypharmacy in Elderly." *Expert Opinion on Drug Safety* 13.1 (2014): 57-65. Print.

Mazidi, M., et al. "The Effect of Hydroalcoholic Extract of Cannabiis Sativa on Appetite Hormone in Rat." *Journal of Complementary and Integrative Medicine.* 11.4 (2014): 253-57. Web.

Micale, V., and Drago, F. "Endocannabinoid System, Stress and Hpa Axis." *European Journal of Pharmacology* 834 (2018): 230-39. Print.

Mondino, A., et al. "Vaporized Cannabis Differentially Modulates Sexual Behavior of Female Rats According to the Dose." *Pharmacology, Biochemistry, and Behavior* (2019). Print.

Monte, A.A., et al. "Acute Illness Associated with Cannabis Use, by Route of Exposure: An Observational Study." *Annals of Internal Medicine* 170.8 (2019): 531-37. Print.

Moreno-Sanz, G. "Can You Pass the Acid Test? Critical Review and Novel Therapeutic Perspectives of Δ9-Tetrahydrocannabinolic Acid A." *Cannabis and Cannabinoid Research* 1.1 (2016): 124-30. Print.

Natale, B.V., et al. "Δ9-Tetrahydrocannabinol Exposure During Rat Pregnancy Leads to Symmetrical Fetal Growth Restriction and

Labyrinth-Specific Vascular Defects in the Placenta." *Scientific Reports* 10.1 (2020): 544. Print.

Ngian, G., et al. "The Use of Opioids in Fibromyalgia." *International journal of rheumatic diseases* 14 (2011): 6-11. Print.

Ngueta, G., and Ndjaboue, R. "Lifetime Marijuana Use in Relation to Insulin Resistance in Lean, Overweight, and Obese Us Adults." *Journal of Diabetes* 12.1 (2020): 38-47. Print.

Palomares, B., et al. "Tetrahydrocannabinolic Acid a (Thca-a) Reduces Adiposity and Prevents Metabolic Disease Caused by Diet-Induced Obesity." *Biochemical Pharmacology* 171 (2020): 113693. Print.

Parekh, T., et al. "Marijuana Use among Young Adults (18–44 Years of Age) and Risk of Stroke: A Behavioral Risk Factor Surveillance System Survey Analysis." *Stroke* 51 (2019): 308-10. Print.

Pertwee, R G. "The Diverse Cb1 and Cb2 Receptor Pharmacology of Three Plant Cannabinoids: Δ9-Tetrahydrocannabinol, Cannabidiol and Δ9-Tetrahydrocannabivarin." *The British Journal of Pharmacology* 153.2 (2008): 199-215. Print.

Pertwee, R. G. "The Ring Test: A Quantitative Method for Assessing the "Cataleptic" Effect of Cannabis in Mice." *British Journal of Pharmacology* 46.4 (1972): 753-63. Print.

Rohof, W.O., et al. "Localization of Mglur5, Gabab, Gabaa, and Cannabinoid Receptors on the Vago-Vagal Reflex Pathway Responsible for Transient Lower Esophageal Sphincter Relaxation in Humans: An Immunohistochemical Study." *Journal of Neurogastroenterology and Motility* 24.4 (2012): 383-e173. Print.

Sarne, Y. "Beneficial and Deleterious Effects of Cannabinoids in the Brain: The Case of Ultra-Low Dose Thc." *The American Journal of Drug and Alcohol Abuse* 45.6 (2019): 551-62. Print.

Sherman, K.E., et al. "Human Immunodeficiency Virus and Liver Disease: An Update." *Hepatology (Baltimore, Md.)* 62.6 (2015): 1871-82. Print.

Silva-Cruz, A., et al. "Dual Influence of Endocannabinoids on Long-Term Potentiation of Synaptic Transmission." *Frontiers in Pharmacology* 8 (2017): 921. Print.

Stanley, J. "The Surprising Story of Medical Marijuana and Pediatric Epilepsy." *TEDxBoulder*. TEDx Talks, 2013. Web.

Tan WC, Lo C, Jong A, et al. Marijuana and chronic obstructive lung disease: a population-based study. *CMAJ*. 2009;180(8):814–820. doi:10.1503/cmaj.081040

Tashkin DP. Does smoking marijuana increase the risk of chronic obstructive pulmonary disease?. *CMAJ*. 2009;180(8):797–798. doi:10.1503/cmaj.090142

Timna, N., et al. "Cannabis Induces a Clinical Response in Patients with Crohn's Disease: A Prospective Placebo-Controlled Study." *Clinical Gastroenterology and Hepatology* 11 (2013): 1276-80. Print.

Wyatt, C.M. "Kidney Disease and Hiv Infection." *Topics in Antiviral Medicine* 25.1 (2017): 13-16. Print.